BIBLE WORDS CROSSWORD PUZZLES 2

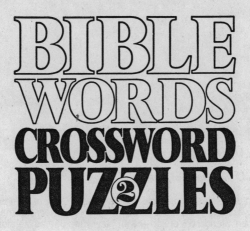

BIBLE WORDS CROSSWORD PUZZLES 2

MARVIN KANANEN

BAKER BOOK HOUSE
Grand Rapids, Michigan 49516

ISBN: 0-8010-5275-0

Third printing, March 1992

Printed in the United States of America

The King James Version of the Bible has been used to prepare most of the puzzle clues. Other versions used are the Living Bible (LB), New International Version (NIV), American Standard Version (ASV), New King James Version (NKJ), Good News Bible (GNB),New English Bible (NEB).

The fifty crossword puzzles in this book
are purposely designed
to help the users uncover Bible truths
as they solve the puzzle clues.
Approximately 75 percent of the clues
are based on Scripture references. Solutions are placed
at the back of the book.
Happy puzzling!

1

Across

1. ___ gave names to all cattle. (Gen. 2:20)
5. Doth Job fear ___ for nought? (Job 1:9)
8. A broad, thick piece.
12. Call me not Naomi, call me ___. (Ruth 1:20)
13. A tree to be desired to make ___ wise. (Gen. 3:6)
14. The ___, because he chews the cud. (Lev. 11:6)
15. Bunah, and ___, and Ozem. (1 Chron. 2:25)
16. To contend with.
17. Shammah the son of ___. (2 Sam. 23:11)
18. The posture of one standing.
20. God accepteth no man's ___. (Gal. 2:6)
22. Continental abbreviation.
23. Receiving the ___ of your faith, even the salvation of your souls. (1 Peter 1:9)
24. Sarai was ___; she had no child. (Gen. 11:30)
27. ___ my soul from their destruction. (Ps. 35:17)
31. ___ the son of Ikkesh the Tekoite. (2 Sam. 23:26)
32. Hanani the seer came to ___. (2 Chron. 16:7)
33. To lower in rank.
37. Even so the tongue is a little ___. (James 3:5)
40. Ye shall have tribulation ___ days. (Rev. 2:10)
41. Bezaleel the son of ___. (Exod. 31:2)
42. Eve because she was the ___ of all living. (Gen. 3:20)
45. Determined to send ___ unto the brethren. (Acts 11:29)
49. To the sheltered side.
50. But [John] confessed, ___ [2 words] not the Christ. (John 1:20)
52. Their visage is blacker than a ___. (Lam. 4:8)
53. To make withered.
54. French vineyard.
55. Porch.
56. French out.
57. Scottish fog.
58. What is this that thou ___ done? (Gen. 3:13)

Down

1. The herdsman prophet.
2. It shall be stoned, or thrust through with a ___. (Heb. 12:20)
3. They are to light the ___ in front of the lampstand. (Num. 8:2, NIV)
4. Ye shall eat no ___ of fat, of ox. (Lev. 7:23)
5. Dost thou now ___ the kingdom of Israel? (1 Kings 21:7)
6. She called his name Ben-___, but his father called him Benjamin. (Gen. 35:18)
7. ___ than hell; what canst thou know? (Job 11:8)
8. You shall drink and drain it, you shall break its ___. (Ezek. 23:34, NKJ)
9. Falls behind.
10. Mars (comb. form).
11. Stood a lamb as it had ___ slain. (Rev. 5:6)
19. A reminder.
21. Direction: Jerusalem to Amman [43 miles].
24. ___ me come unto thee on the water. (Matt. 14:28)
25. Lo-Ammi; for ye ___ not my people. (Hos. 1:9)
26. Elihu the son of Barachel the Buzite, of the kindred of ___. (Job. 32:2)
28. The fourth part of a ___ of dove's dung. (2 Kings 6:25)
29. ___ hospitality one to another. (1 Peter 4:9)
30. O Lord, give ___ to supplications. (Ps. 143:1)

4

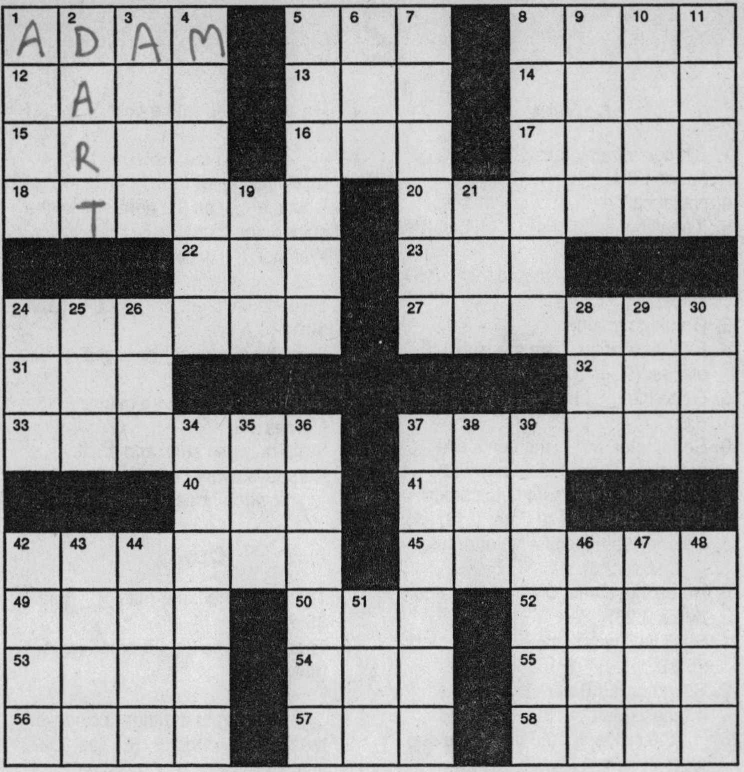

34. And ___ save with fear, pulling them out of the fire. (Jude 23)
35. Ball stand.
36. Thou didst ___ the kings of the earth. (Ezek. 27:33)
37. ___not among yourselves. (John 6:43)
38. Sir, come down ___ my child die. (John 4:49)
39. The name of Nabor's wife, ___. (Gen. 11:29)
42. Uz, and Hul, and Gether, and ___. (Gen. 10:23)
43. Oil (comb. form).
44. Your kerchiefs also will I ___. (Ezek. 13:21)
46. Argyll isle.
47. If a man ___ of this bread, he will live forever. (John 6:51, NIV)
48. A blind man, or a lame, or he that hath a ___ nose. (Lev. 21:18)
51. Jephunneh, and Pispah, and ___. (1 Chron. 7:38)

2

Across

1. Sin is the transgression of the ___. (1 John 3:4)
4. Naval call.
8. It shall not fasten its ___ on me. (Ps. 101:3, ASV)
12. Direction: Jerusalem to Jericho [15 miles].
13. Greek commune.
14. He made him ___ on the high places. (Deut. 32:13)
15. Go to the ___, thou sluggard. (Prov. 6:6)
16. She trusted not in the LORD; she ___ not near to her God. (Zeph. 3:2)
17. Their ___ of pleasure is to carouse in broad daylight. (2 Peter 2:13, NIV)
18. He shewed himself alive after his ___. (Acts 1:3)
20. He cannot stand, but hath ___ end. (Mark 3:26)
21. Shall vain words have an ___. (Job 16:3)
22. Simon called Peter, and ___ his brother. (Matt. 4:18)
26. ___the sickle, for the harvest is ripe. (Joel 3:13, NIV)
29. Go and ___ where he is, that I may send and fetch him. (2 Kings 6:13)
30. One shot or one spot.
31. Even the ___ went in after the blade. (Judg. 3:22, NKJ)
32. Lot ___ in the gate of Sodom. (Gen. 19:1)
33. Turkish commander.
34. Palm leaf.
35. ___the tree down, and destroy it. (Dan. 4:23)
36. Jewish hell.
37. Then returned they unto Jerusalem from the mount called ___. (Acts 1:12)
39. Large primate.
40. I ___ made all things to all men. (1 Cor. 9:22)
41. Where is the ___ of his coming? (2 Peter 3:4)
45. He was armed with a coat of ___. (1 Sam. 17:5)
48. ___ not upon me, because I am black. (Song of Sol. 1:6)
49. Cast the ___ on the right side of the ship. (John 21:6)
50. Was not ___ Jacob's brother? (Mal. 1:2)
51. Give me children, or ___ I die. (Gen. 30:1)
52. Were there not ___ cleansed? (Luke 17:17)
53. But the tongue can no man ___. (James 3:8)
54. State between child and adult.
55. Cursed is every one that hangeth ___ [2 words] tree. (Gal. 3:13)

Down

1. Then shall the lame man ___. (Isa. 35:6)
2. There was one ___, a prophetess. (Luke 2:36)
3. Moistens.
4. ___one thing to another to discover the scheme of things. (Eccles. 7:27, NIV)
5. Pilate and ___ were made friends. (Luke 23:12)
6. To seek an ___, he will cast lots. (Ezek. 21:21, NIV).
7. Coniferous tree.
8. He [Samson] did ___ in the prison house. (Judg. 16:21)
9. I will ___ you out of their bondage. (Exod. 6:6)
10. Chemical suffix.
11. A podded vine.
19. The father ___ the Son to be the Saviour. (1 John 4:14)
20. If ___ of you lack wisdom, let him ask of God. (James 1:5)
22. Be gentle unto all men, ___ to teach, patient. (2 Tim. 2:24)
23. Why did the heathen ___? (Acts 4:25)

6

24. Reflected sound.
25. State of prosperity.
26. A driving sound.
27. If the Lord ___, we shall live. (James 4:15)
28. ___, the Ahohite. (1 Chron. 11:29)
29. I ___ three unclean spirits like frogs. (Rev. 16:13)
32. I will ___ my face against that man. (Lev. 20:3)
33. Throat clearing sound.
35. A woman . . . touched the ___ of his garment. (Matt. 9:20)
36. Let not then your good be evil ___ of. (Rom. 14:16)
38. Ye are of more ___ than many sparrows. (Luke 12:7)

39. Jonah ___ and went unto Nineveh. (Jonah 3:3)
41. Make thee a fiery serpent, and set it upon a ___. (Num. 21:8)
42. They shall not enter ___ my rest. (Heb. 3:11)
43. Write the things which thou hast ___. (Rev. 1:19)
44. Sicilian volcano.
45. Mercy and truth are ___ together. (Ps. 85:10)
46. Then ___ was wroth with the seer. (2 Chron. 16:10)
47. Because I said, ___ [2 words] the Son of God. (John 10:36)
48. ___ us be glad and rejoice. (Rev. 19:7)

3

Across

1. Alpha follower.
5. ___ the harlot, yet let not Judah offend. (Hos. 4:15)
9. How long ___ is it since this came unto him? (Mark 9:21)
12. Of the sons also of ___, Ebed. (Ezra 8:6)
13. What does this ___ mean to you? (Exod. 12:26, ASV)
14. Why then doth their king inherit ___? (Jer. 49:1)
15. Giving heed to seducing spirits and ___ of demons. (1 Tim. 4:1)
17. The serpent first beguiled ___. (2 Cor. 11:3)
18. Pompeii character.
19. This man shall be blessed in his ___. (James 1:25)
20. To bring to light.
23. Samuel feared to show ___ the vision. (1 Sam. 3:15)
25. Ten ___ are a homer. (Ezek. 45:14)
26. Even leviathan that ___ serpent. (Isa. 27:1)
30. He came and touched the ___. (Luke 7:14)
31. We sailed to the ___ of Crete. (Acts 27:7, NIV)
32. Hired transportation.
33. Their ___ and Pharisees murmured. (Luke 5:30)
35. Whoever ___ to keep his life will lose it. (Luke 17:33, NIV)
36. Behold, a throne was ___ in heaven. (Rev. 4:2)
37. People of France.
38. An he goat came from the ___. (Dan. 8:5)
41. Will not pain ___ you? (Jer. 13:21, NIV)
42. An adulteress . . . says, "___ done nothing wrong." (Prov. 30:20, NIV)
43. The ___ [2 words] also is witness to us. (Heb. 10:15)
48. Ye have made it a ___ of thieves. (Luke 19:46)
49. Arrow poison.
50. ___, lama sabacthani? (Mark 15:34)
51. The ___ of all things is at hand. (1 Peter 4:7)
52. If any be a hearer of the word, and not a ___. (James 1:23)
53. I have ___ sackcloth over my skin. (Job 16:15, NKJ)

Down

1. Come unto Jerusalem, building the rebellious and the ___ city. (Ezra 4:12)
2. Old Tokyo.
3. Spasmodic contraction.
4. He is ___, that denieth the Father. (1 John 2:22)
5. In his hands the ___ of nails. (John 20:25)
6. Judgment also will I lay to the ___. (Isa. 28:17)
7. I ___ no pleasant bread. (Dan. 10:3)
8. ___, of the Gentiles also. (Rom. 3:29)
9. Shammah the son of ___. (2 Sam. 23:11)
10. I ___ her space to repent. (Rev. 2:21)
11. Azariat the son of ___. (2 Chron. 15:1)
16. Kings (French).
19. ___, who loveth to have the preeminence. (3 John 9)
20. Now my life ___ away. (Job 30:16, NIV)
21. Secular.
22. Roman road.
23. ___ the lamp of God went out. (1 Sam. 3:3)
24. ___, in her mouth was an olive leaf. (Gen. 8:11)
26. French pronoun.
27. Cain (German).

28. Manager's abbreviation.
29. He that dippeth his hand with me in the ___. (Matt. 26:23)
31. ___ us be glad and rejoice. (Rev. 19:7)
34. They shall ___ driven to darkness. (Isa. 8:22)
35. Tidy or firm.
37. One who fries.
38. The land was ___, and quiet. (1 Chron. 4:40)
39. Reward her ___ as she rewarded you. (Rev. 18:6)

40. I ___ my messenger before thy face. (Mark 1:2)
41. I stumbled, they gathered in ___. (Ps. 35:15, NIV)
43. Adam and his wife ___ themselves. (Gen. 3:8)
44. The children of Lod, Hadd, and ___. (Neh. 7:37)
45. Bullfight cheer.
46. Sir, didst not thou ___ good seed? (Matt. 13:27)
47. Purge away thy dross, and take away all thy ___. (Isa. 1:25)

4

Across

1. ___, and Dumah, and Eshean. (Josh. 15:52)
5. Jesus entered the temple ___. (Matt. 21:12, NIV)
9. He ___ shown his people the power of his works. (Ps. 111:6, NIV)
12. Average.
13. Coarse Asian sugar.
14. Why make ye this ___, and weep? (Mark 5:39)
15. One of the twelve.
17. When I became a ___, I put away childish things. (1 Cor. 13:11)
18. Let us search and ___ our ways. (Lam. 3:40)
19. The similitude of ___ transgression. (Rom. 5:14)
21. Therefore put on the full ___ of God. (Eph. 6:13, NIV)
24. I looked, and behold, an ___ horse. (Rev. 6:8, ASV)
26. Typical standard.
27. Babism off-shoot.
28. ___ to now, ye rich men, and weep. (John 5:1)
30. Plural pronoun (Latin).
31. Navigational system.
32. They shall give unto the priest the shoulder, and the two cheeks, and the ___. (Deut. 18:3)
33. Say Amen ___ thy giving of thanks. (1 Cor. 14:16)
34. Predatory claw.
35. A people great, and many, and ___, as the Anakims. (Deut. 2:10)
36. Set of twelve.
37. This ___ for a mind with wisdom. (Rev. 17:9, NIV)
38. Great is ___ of the Ephesians. (Acts 19:28)
40. Riblah, on the east side of ___. (Num. 34:11)
41. I have broken the ___ of Pharaoh. (Ezek. 30:21)
42. They received the word with all ___. (Acts 17:11)
48. As the lad ___, he shot an arrow. (1 Sam. 20:36)
49. The Pharisees began to ___ him. (Luke 11:53)
50. Woe to them that are at ___ in Zion. (Amos 6:1)
51. Prussian spa town.
52. Amos, O thou ___, go, flee thee away. (Amos 7:12)
53. His tail ___ the third part of the stars of heaven. (Rev. 12:4)

Down

1. The dumb ___ speaking with man's voice. (2 Peter 2:16)
2. Deliver thyself as a ___ from the hand of the hunter. (Prov. 6:5)
3. The sucking child shall play on the hole of the ___. (Isa. 11:8)
4. They sank into the ___ as a stone. (Exod. 15:5)
5. Then came I with an ___, and rescued him. (Acts 23:27)
6. Jewish master.
7. Zoology (comb. form).
8. ___ fell upon his face, and laughed. (Gen. 17:17)
9. So they hanged ___ on the gallows. (Esther 7:10)
10. ___ was not deceived. (1 Tim. 2:14)
11. Beloved, now we are the ___ of God. (1 John 3:2)
16. They ___ in vision, they stumble in judgment. (Isa. 28:7)
20. The gods (Latin).
21. There was one ___, a prophetess. (Luke 2:36)
22. The love of money is the ___ of all evil. (1 Tim. 6:10)
23. Singular of Mmes.
24. Saying unto ___, Make us gods to go before us. (Acts 7:40)

25. Took the body of Saul and the bodies of his sons from the wall of Beth-___. (1 Sam. 31:12)
27. Tree trunk.
28. Ye have turned judgment into ___. (Amos 6:12)
29. I am a brother to dragons, and a companion to ___. (Job 30:29)
31. ___, come forth. (John 11:43)
32. Evil (prefix).
34. A long one equals 2,240 pounds.
35. I am dark because the sun ___ me. (Song of Sol.1:6, NKJ)
36. Condemns everlastingly.
37. 102 (Roman).

38. None is so fierce that ___ stir him. (Job. 41:10)
39. Duke Magdiel, Duke ___: these be the dukes of Edom. (Gen. 36:43)
40. Zebadiah, and Arad, and ___. (1 Chron. 8:15)
43. How long will it be ___ ye make an end of words? (Job 18:2)
44. He is of ___; ask him. (John 9:23)
45. First the blade, then the ___ (Mark 4:28)
46. Direction: Jerusalem to Masada [34 miles].
47. A time to rend and a time to ___. (Eccles. 3:7)

5

Across

1. Toss thee like a ___ into a large country. (Isa. 22:18)
5. Israel ___ this song, Spring up, O well. (Num. 21:17)
9. There was again a battle in ___ with the Philistines. (2 Sam. 21:19)
12. The diviners have seen ___ [2 words]. (Zech. 10:2)
13. The churches in ___ salute you. (1 Cor. 16:19)
14. ___ no man anything, but to love one another. (Rom. 13:8)
15. California rockfish.
16. Swerve.
17. That ___ serpent, which is the Devil. (Rev. 20:2)
18. Egyptian name for the Red Sea.
20. Neither ___ we eat any man's bread. (2 Thess. 3:8)
22. Eyes (Scottish).
23. Dog shelter.
26. Like that of a ___ that has stopped its ears. (Ps. 58:4, NIV)
29. He will silence her noisy ___. (Jer. 51:55, NIV)
30. Direction: Jaffa to Jericho.
31. Take heed that ye despise not one of these little ___. (Matt. 18:10)
32. A brother offended is harder to be ___. (Prov. 18:19)
33. Slap sharply.
34. Greenland Eskimo.
35. I said unto him, ___, thou knowest. (Rev. 7:14)
36. Even so, come, Lord ___. (Rev. 22:20)
37. Did we eat any man's bread for ___? (2 Thess. 3:8)
39. Extinct large ratite bird.
40. Such knowledge is ___ wonderful for me. (Ps. 139:6)
41. For the Son of man is Lord even of the ___ day. (Matt. 12:8)
45. Samuel feared to show ___ the vision. (1 Sam. 3:15)
47. In a vision, and I was by the river of ___. (Dan. 8:2)
49. Ohio's Great Lake.
50. As for all the hills once cultivated by the ___. (Isa. 7:25, NIV)
51. Friend, ___ me three loaves.
52. Between a viscount and a marquis.
53. That which groweth of ___ own accord. (Lev. 25:5)
54. The ___ shall eat Jezebel. (2 Kings 9:10)
55. Go to the ___ and buy some for yourselves. (Matt. 25:9, NEB)

Down

1. Elephantine cry.
2. To the protected side.
3. Judgment also will I lay to the ___. (Isa. 28:17)
4. They be blind ___ of the blind. (Matt. 15:14)
5. He ___ the needy from the sword. (Job 5:15 NIV)
6. Am I ___ [2 words], or a whale? (Job 7:12)
7. Old English eyes.
8. Did not I see thee in the ___? (John 18:26)
9. As cold waters to a thirsty soul, so is ___ [2 words] from a far country. (Prov. 25:25)
10. I am like an ___ of the desert. (Ps. 102:6)
11. Take up thy ___ and walk. (John 5:11)
19. Israel saw the Egyptians dead upon the ___ shore. (Exod. 14:30)
21. While ye have light, believe ___ the light. (John 12:36)
23. If any of his ___ come to redeem it, then shall he. (Lev. 25:25)
24. ___ was a cunning hunter. (Gen. 25:27)
25. Under the whole heaven He ___ it [thunder] loose. (Job 37:3, ASV)

26. Show me the ___ used for paying the tax. (Matt. 22:19, NIV)
27. It [the fish] vomited Jonah up ___ the dry land. (Jonah 2:10, ASV)
28. In the ___ of holiness from the womb of the morning. (Ps. 110:3)
29. The son of Abinadab, in all the region of ___. (1 Kings 4:11)
32. To ___, that God was in Christ. (2 Cor. 5:19)
33. Navy's construction personnel.
35. It is not good that the man ___ be alone. (Gen. 2:18)
36. Doth ___ fear God for nought? (Job 1:9)

38. Let not the sun ___ down on your wrath. (Eph. 4:26)
39. Mine house and my ___ count me for a stranger. (Job 19:15)
41. Then believed they his words; they ___ his praise. (Ps. 106:12)
42. The sons of Ulla; ___, and Haniel, and Rezia. (1 Chron. 7:39)
43. Novice.
44. I will make him an ___ meet for him. (Gen. 2:18)
45. ___ and Rosh, Muppim and Huppim, and Ard. (Gen. 46:21)
46. Haran begat ___.
48. 45th pope (440-461).

6

Across

1. ___ to teach. (1 Tim. 3:2)
4. The king called to ___, Saul's servant. (2 Sam. 9:9)
8. Thou shalt not ___ upon usury. (Deut. 23:9)
12. Until the day that ___ entered into the ark. (Luke 17:27)
13. In the ___ that is called Patmos. (Rev. 1:9)
14. Forbidden of the Holy Ghost to preach the word in ___. (Acts 16:6)
15. The dumb ___ speaking with man's voice. (2 Peter 2:16)
16. Milalai, Gilalai, ___, Nethaneel and Judah. (Neh. 12:36)
17. Without (French).
18. The sons of ___, Abraham's concubine. (1 Chron. 1:32)
20. The daughter of ___, Abraham's concubine. (1 Chron. 1:32)
21. Pouch.
22. Said I, ___ is me! for I am undone. (Isa. 6:5)
23. Melchizedek king of ___. (Gen. 14:18)
26. She [Keturah] bare Zimram and ___. (Gen. 25:2)
30. Utmost hyperbole.
31. Unclean for you: the weasel, the ___, any kind of lizard. (Lev. 11:29, NIV)
32. How long will it be ___ thou be quiet? (Jer. 47:6)
33. Sara obeyed ___, calling him lord. (1 Peter 3:6)
36. The ___ saw it, and feared. (Isa. 41:5)
38. Their brethren of the second degree, Zechariah, ___, and Jaaziel. (1 Chron. 15:18)
39. Peer Gynt's mother
40. She bare him Zimran, and Jokshan, and ___. (Gen. 25:2)
43. Hagar bare ___ to Abram. (Gen. 16:16)
47. Mattathias, which was the son of ___. (Luke 3:25)
48. Observe the month of ___, and keep the passover. (Deut. 16:1)
49. To possess (Scottish).
50. He must do so according to the ___ of the Passover. (Num. 9:14, NKJ)
51. Life (Spanish).
52. Hanai the seer came to ___. (2 Chron. 16:7)
53. Saints abbreviation.
54. The name of the well ___; because they strove with him. (Gen. 26:20)
55. His cheeks are as a ___ of spices. (Song of Sol. 5:13)

Down

1. We saw the giants, the sons of ___. (Num. 13:33)
2. Let me ___ a riddle to you. (Judg. 14:12, NKJ)
3. Do not ___ the LORD your God. (Deut. 6:16, NIV)
4. She [Keturah] bare him [Abraham] ___. (Gen. 25:2)
5. Take now thy son, thine only son ___. (Gen. 22:2)
6. Term of disgust.
7. First vowels.
8. A rebuke impresses . . . more than a hundred ___ a fool. (Prov. 17:10, NIV)
9. ___ was a cunning hunter. (Gen. 25:27)
10. Columbus caravel.
11. Thou shalt ___ them in pieces. (Ps. 2:9)
19. In vain shalt thou ___ many medicines. (Jer. 46:11)
20. Siamese measure.
22. ___ ye not what the scripture saith? (Rom. 11:2)
23. The new heaven and first earth were passed away; and there was no more ___. (Rev. 21:1)

24. Priestly garment.
25. Tutelary god.
26. Sugary preserve.
27. Underworld goddess of the dead.
28. The vocation wherewith ye ___ called. (Eph. 4:1)
29. Cape.
31. And Philip ___ thither to him. (Acts 8:30)
34. Humbles.
35. As a ___ doth gather her brood. (Luke 13:34)
36. Medan, and Midian, and ___, and Shuah. (Gen. 25:2)
37. ___, which was the son of Noe. (Luke 3:36)

39. Wherefore laying ___ all malice. (1 Peter 2:1)
40. Paul stood in the midst of ___ hill. (Acts 17:22)
41. The canals will ___ a stench. (Isa. 19:6, ASV)
42. A sword is upon the liars; and they shall ___. (Jer. 50:36)
43. Egyptian wading bird.
44. ___ the son of Omri did evil. (1 Kings 16:30)
45. Tremble, ye women that are at ___. (Isa. 32:11)
46. I will ___ on softly. (Gen. 33:14)
48. Rosary bead.

7

Across

1. Low voice or fish.
5. I am not ____, most noble Festus. (Acts 26:25)
8. Your ____ have a pleasing fragrance. (Song of Sol. 1:3, NIV)
12. Without an ____ he was made priest. (Heb. 7:20)
13. Lod, and ____, the valley of craftsmen. (Neh. 11:35)
14. Russian mountain range.
15. Of or belonging to the planet Mars.
16. Eyes full of ____, and that cannot cease. (2 Peter 2:14)
18. Before ____ thou shalt become a plain. (Zech 4:7)
20. ____ king of Hamath. (2 Sam. 8:9)
21. Ten curtains of fine ____ linen. (Exod. 26:1)
25. High card.
28. Sweetsop.
30. That they may recover themselves out of the ____ of the devil. (2 Tim. 2:26)
31. To restrain.
33. Double curve.
35. Irish free estate.
36. Warble.
38. Go and ____ where he is, that I may send and fetch him. (2 Kings 6:13)
40. Leary drug of choice.
41. Men from every language of the nations shall grasp the ____ of a Jewish man. (Zech. 8:23 NKJV)
43. To him that overcometh will I give to ____ of the hidden manna. (Rev. 2:17)
45. ____ saith unto him, LORD, not my feet only. (John 13:9)
50. We also are men of like ____ with you. (Acts 14:15)
53. No man might buy or sell, ____ he that had the mark. (Rev. 13:17)
54. Appoint over you terror, consumption, and the burning ____. (Lev. 26:16)
55. Twentieth English letter.
56. How soon is the fig ____ withered. (Matt. 21:20)
57. The diligent ____ only to plenteousness. (Prov. 21:5)
58. Ye do ____, not knowing the scriptures. (Matt. 22:29)
59. He shall ____ his angel before thee. (Gen. 24:7)

Down

1. Salmon begat ____. (Ruth 4:21)
2. Swiss river.
3. Conditional suffix.
4. The LORD himself shall descend from heaven with a ____. (1 Thess 4:16)
5. The ____ should not come into the congregation of God for ever. (Neh. 13:1)
6. ____ [2 words] crown was given unto him. (Rev. 6:2)
7. No ____ this man is a murderer. (Acts 28:4)
8. With a line and makes an ____ with a marker. (Isa. 44:13 NIV)
9. Wrath.
10. Monkey.
11. A ____ tongue brings angry looks. (Prov. 25:23)
17. Bulgarian coins or men's names.
19. Snake, feathery or otherwise.
22. Leave us a remnant to escape, and to give us a ____ in his holy place. (Ezra 9:8)
23. He who makes haste with his feet ____. (Prov. 19:2)
24. To make the Gentiles obedient, by word and ____. (Rom. 15:18)
25. Man shall speak of the might of thy terrible ____. (Ps. 145:6)
26. Spiral shape.
27. Great Lake.
29. Balaam smote the ____. (Num. 22:23)

32. Ezra _____ the LORD, the great God. (Neh. 8:5)
34. Author of The Fairie Queen.
37. Fifty-seven (Roman).
39. To bark shrilly.
42. Theatrical sentiment.
44. The LORD _____ the heart. (Prov. 17:3, NIV)
46. Unique person.
47. The devil threw him down, and _____ him. (Luke 9:42)

48. When the _____ was come, he sat down with the twelve. (Matt. 26:20)
49. A bruised _____ shall he not break. (Isa. 42:3)
50. A light slap.
51. He is of _____; ask him. (John 9:21)
52. The _____ became black as sackcloth. (Rev. 6:12)

8

Across

1. This man welcomes sinners and ___ with them. (Luke 15:2, NIV)
5. Thou ___ not Caesar's friend. (John 19:12)
8. They break their bones, and ___ them in pieces. (Mic. 3:3)
12. The son of Paul's sister heard of this ___. (Acts 23:16, NIV)
13. As the days of ___ were, so shall also the coming of the Son of man be. (Matt. 24:37)
14. As the camel, and the ___, and the coney. (Deut. 14:7)
15. A ship of Alexandria which had wintered in the ___. (Acts. 28:11)
16. ___, woe is unto me if I preach not the gospel! (1 Cor. 9:16)
17. Israel shouted with a great shout, so that the earth ___ again. (1 Sam. 4:5)
18. Ancient scriptural manuscript.
20. He taught them as one having authority, and not as the ___. (Matt. 7:29)
22. How is the gold become ___! (Lam. 4:1)
24. I will give to everyone according to what he ___ done. (Rev. 22:12, NIV)
25. To restore and to build Jerusalem unto the ___. (Dan. 9:25)
29. Let us set for him there a bed, and a table, and a ___. (2 Kings 4:10)
33. ___thought she had been drunken. (1 Sam. 1:13)
34. Their foolish heart ___ darkened. (Rom. 1:21)
36. Bodily nucleic acid.
37. Small pies.
40. The ___ of God is nigh at hand. (Luke 21: 31)
43. The name of the wicked shall ___. (Prov. 10:7)
45. Thou art lukewarm, and neither cold ___ hot. (Rev. 3:16)
46. Children that will not lie: so he was their ___. (Isa. 63:8)

50. Touch not; ___ not; handle not. (Col. 2:21)
54. ___ told Jezebel all that Elijah had done. (1 Kings 19:1)
55. Strike lightly.
57. Surely there is a ___ for the silver. (Job. 28:1)
58. Who is this that rises like the ___? (Jer. 46:7, NIV)
59. Peruvian oxalis.
60. Within (prefix).
61. ___ not the very nature of things teach you? (1 Cor. 11:14, NIV)
62. Eat not of it ___, nor sodden. (Exod. 12:9)
63. Mary and Elizabeth, e.g.

Down

1 A grand tale.
2. That I say come and worship him ___. (Matt. 2:8)
3. He ___ me all that ever I did. (John 4:39)
4. Galloping, galloping go his mighty ___. (Judg. 5:22, NIV)
5. No man hath seen God at ___ time. (1 John 4:12)
6. Were as swift as the ___ upon the mountains. (1 Chron. 12:8)
7. A prophetess, to ___ and seduce my servants. (Rev. 2:20)
8. Thou art the ___. (Matt. 16:16)
9. Mayan year.
10. Wine measure.
11. Do they make ___ from it [the vine] to hang things on? (Ezek. 15:3, NIV)
19. Roman number of disciples.
21. Ethiopian title.
23. Give unto the priest the shoulder, and the two cheeks, and the ___. (Deut. 18:3)
25. In that place where Martha ___ him. (John 11:30)
26. Utmost hyperbole.
27. I said unto him, ___, thou knowest. (Rev. 7:14)

28. Indian due.

30. Money, wherewith the ___ number of them is to be redeemed. (Num. 3:48)

31. ___, the valley of craftsmen. (Neh. 11:35)

32. Loom lever.

35. ___ shall have great pain, and No shall be rent. (Ezek. 30:16)

38. Ye also shall sit . . . judging the twelve ___ of Israel. (Matt. 19:28)

39. River rapids.

41. Without him was ___ anything made. (John 1:3)

42. All that are in the ___ shall hear his voice. (John 5:28)

44. The law was our ___ to bring us to Christ. (Gal. 3:24, NKJ)

46. A foolish man, which built his house upon ___. (Matt. 7:26)

47. Uzzah and ___, sons of Abinadab. (2 Sam. 6:3)

48. The ___ of Siddim was full of slimepits. (Gen. 14:10)

49. Whosoever shall say to his brother ___ shall be in danger. (Matt. 5:22)

51. These twelve Jesus ___ forth. (Matt. 10:5)

52. And behold at evening ___ trouble. (Isa. 17:14)

53. ___, which was the son of Seth. (Luke 3:38)

56. The LORD that delivered me out of the ___ of the lion. (1 Sam. 17:37)

9

Across

1. Be silent, O ___ flesh, before the LORD. (Zech. 2:13)
4. He burned the bones of the king of Edom into ___. (Amos 2:1)
8. They ___ out swords from their lips. (Ps. 59:7, NIV)
12. The hills once cultivated by the ___. (Isa. 7:25, NIV)
13. Old Irish garment.
14. Now I would not ___ you ignorant. (Rom. 1:3)
15. Thou shalt not covet . . . his ox, nor his ___. (Exod. 20:17)
16. Judas begat Phares and ___. (Matt. 1:3)
17. Of ___, the family of the Eranites. (Num. 26:36)
18. Jesus six days before the passover came to ___. (John 12:1)
20. Brought men from Babylon, and from Cuthah, and from ___. (2 Kings 17:24)
21. Tempted like as we ___, yet without sin. (Heb. 4:15)
22. I will make Rabbah a ___ for camels. (Ezek. 25:5)
25. Joab took Amasa by the ___. (2 Sam. 20:9)
28. Upon the great ___ of their right foot. (Exod. 29:20)
29. Gold coin.
30. ___, Father, all things are possible unto thee. (Mark 14:36)
31. Her ___ was to light on a part of the field belonging to Boaz. (Ruth 2:3)
32. With what measure ye ___, it shall be measured to you. (Matt. 7:2)
33. Third letter.
34. Smote them, until they came under Beth-___. (1 Sam. 7:11)
35. They drew ___ and certain brethren unto the rulers of the city. (Acts 17:6)
36. ___ poison is under their lips. (Ps. 140:3)

38. Aaron thy brother died in mount ___. (Deut. 32:50)
39. He said, ___; but thou didst laugh. (Gen. 18:15)
40. ___ in the highest. (Matt. 21:9)
44. Irish tenant.
46. You will be protected from the ___ of the tongue. (Job 5:21, NIV)
47. All that handle the ___, the mariners. (Ezek. 27:29)
48. The children's teeth are set on ___. (Jer. 31:29)
49. Isaac loved ___, because he did eat of his venison. (Gen. 25:28)
50. Medical group.
51. Make thee an ark of gopher ___. (Gen. 6:14)
52. Hebrew measure.
53. And touched the ___ of his garment. (Matt. 9:20)

Down

1. ___ had seventy sons in Samaria. (2 Kings 10:1)
2. He that loveth his life shall ___ it. (John 12:25)
3. Neither shall ye touch it, ___ ye die. (Gen. 3:3)
4. The ___, and the snail, and the mole. (Lev. 11:30)
5. Lacking sense.
6. But ___ kept all these things, and pondered them in her heart. (Luke 2:9)
7. Time division.
8. ___ the father of Machbenah. (1 Chron. 2:49)
9. Why speakest thou unto them in ___? (Matt. 13:10)
10. Evangeline St. Clare's nickname.
11. Having a ___, or scurvy, or scabbed, ye shall not offer these. (Lev. 22:22)
19. Brought them unto Halah, and Habor, and ___. (1 Chron. 5:26)
20. I ___ no pleasant bread. (Dan. 10:3)
22. After the ___ Satan entered into him. (John 13:27)

23. Apollo's mother.

24. Some indeed preach Christ ___ of envy. (Phil. 1:15)

25. Who passing through the valley of ___ make it a well. (Ps. 84:6)

26. Behold, Gaal the son of ___. (Judg. 9:31)

27. Shadrach, Meshach, and ___. (Dan. 2:49)

28. She got a papyrus basket for him and coated it with ___ and pitch. (Exod. 2:3, NIV)

31. He ___ risen! He is not here. (Mark 16:6, NIV)

32. Call me not Naomi, call me ___. (Ruth 1:20)

34. Howl, O gate: ___, O city. (Isa. 14:31)

35. Now ___ was clothed with filthy garments. (Zech. 3:3)

37. The heifer . . . which is neither ___ or sown. (Deut. 21:4)

38. The coast turneth to ___; and the outgoings thereof are at the sea. (Josh. 19:29)

40. Hinged metal latch.

41. Though . . . ___, Daniel, and Job were in it. (Ezek. 14:14)

42. His ___ is called The Word of God. (Rev. 19:13)

43. Balak the king of Moab hath brought me from ___. (Num. 23:7)

44. A time to rend, and a time to ___. (Eccles. 3:7)

45. Why make ye this ___, and weep? (Mark 5:39)

46. We sailed to the ___ of Crete. (Acts 27:7, NIV)

10

Across

1. The ___, whereof thou canst not be healed. (Deut. 28:27)
5. He planted an ___, and the rain doth nourish it. (Isa. 44:14)
8. To smite with the ___ of wickedness. (Isa. 58:4)
12. Tan (German).
13. Every prostitute receives a ___. (Ezek. 16:33, NIV)
14. Saith the LORD, that thou shalt call me ___. (Hos. 2:16)
15. In the time of the month ___ thou camest out of Egypt. (Exod. 34:18)
16. Pure ___ and undefiled before God and the Father. (James 1:27)
18. A fire on Magog, and among them that dwell carelessly in the ___. (Ezek. 39:6)
20. Your ___ shall commit adultery. (Hos. 4:13)
21. When the time of the promise ___ nigh. (Acts 7:17)
23. A third part shall be at the gate of ___. (2 Kings 11:6)
24. With them in the clouds, to meet the Lord in the ___. (1 Thess. 4:17)
26. For I ___ that he whom thou blessest is blessed. (Num. 22:6)
28. Took ___ by war, and called the name of it Joktheel. (2 Kings 14:7)
32. While he yet spake, the cock ___. (Luke 22:60)
34. The kingdom of heaven is like a ___, that was cast into the sea. (Matt. 13:47)
36. ___ obeyed Abraham, calling him lord. (1 Peter 3:6)
37. Light boat.
39. Neither shall the sun light on thee, ___ any heat. (Rev. 7:16)
41. ___ but, O man, who art thou that repliest against God? (Rom. 9:20)
42. Cape Horn native.
44. Where the cloth makers work, by the ditch that brings water from the upper ___. (Isa. 36:2, GNB)
46. She layeth her hands to the ___. (Prov. 31:19)
50. Of birds, and of serpents, and of things in the sea, hath been ___. (James 3:7)
53. Now Joseph was well-built and ___. (Gen. 39:6, NIV)
55. Evil (Spanish).
56. As He has promised, that you shall observe this ___. (Exod. 12:25, ASV)
57. Abner, the son of ___, Saul's uncle. (1 Sam. 14:50)
58. Greek Cupid.
59. Crocus.
60. Survive by great effort.
61. Theatrical sketch.

Down

1. ___ the Ahohite. (1 Chron. 11:29)
2. Whose land is spoken of in Judges 11:5?
3. Ye are of God, little ___. (1 John 4:4)
4. Phalec, which was the son of ___. (Luke 3:35)
5. Continental abbreviation.
6. Thou art a God who ___. (Gen. 16:13, ASV)
7. Gifts of healings, ___, governments. (1 Cor. 12:28)
8. ___ which ye made to worship. (Acts 7:43)
9. Horus' mother.
10. Over Edom will I cast out my ___. (Ps. 60:8)
11. Cans.
17. Notes of obligation.
19. Woe to the women that ___ pillows. (Ezek. 13:18)
22. A brother offended is harder to be ___. (Prov. 18:19)
24. Air coordinating group.
25. ___ the son of Ikkesh the Tekoite. (2 Sam. 23:26).

27. After Abram had dwelt ___ years in the land of Canaan. (Gen. 16:3)
29. Thou shalt not remove thy neighbour's ___. (Deut. 19:14)
30. The sons of Jether; Jephunneh, and Pispah, and ___. (1 Chron. 7:38)
31. The ___ appeareth, and the tender grass sheweth itself. (Prov. 27:25)
33. Have me away, for I am sore ___. (2 Chron. 35:23)
35. I will make thee like the ___ of a rock. (Ezek. 26:14)
38. Thou shouldest be for salvation unto the ___ of the earth. (Acts 13:47)
40. The name of the wicked shall ___. (Prov. 10:7)

43. Let her ___; why trouble ye her? (Mark 14:6)
45. Your ___ are written in heaven. (Luke 10:20)
46. Indian title.
47. He that sat on him had a ___ of balances in his hand. (Rev. 6:5)
48. Inca sun god.
49. Toward the north side of Beth-___, and Neiel. (Josh. 19:27)
51. ___, lama sabacthani? (Mark 15:34)
52. Lord, holy and true, ___ thou not judge? (Rev. 6:10)
54. How long will it be ___ they believe. (Num. 14:11)

11

Across

1. Have ___ in yourselves, and have peace one with another. (Mark 9:50)
5. The ___, and the pelican, and the gier eagle. (Lev. 11:8)
9. With the ___ of an ass have I slain a thousand men. (Judg. 15:16)
12. ___, Muppim, and Huppim. (Gen. 46:21)
13. Die's six.
14. ___ no man any thing, but to love. (Rom. 13:8)
15. For to this end Christ both died, and ___. (Rom. 14:9)
16. I sat not in the ___ of the mockers. (Jer. 15:17)
18. Once more I will ___ these people. (Isa. 29:14 NIV)
20. The face of the Lord is against them that ___ evil. (1 Peter 3:12)
21. Anthony (French).
23. Ye shall hear of ___ and commotions. (Luke 21:9)
27. My father will stop thinking about the donkeys and ___ worrying about us. (1 Sam. 9:5, NIV)
30. Extinct bird.
32. Naphtali is a ___ set free. (Gen. 49:21, NIV)
33. Laddie's beloved.
35. How shall we ___, if we neglect so great salvation. (Heb. 2:3)
37. The sons of ___, Hophni and Phinehas. (1 Sam. 1:3)
38. Shade tree.
40. Came and ___ them into the pot of pottage. (2 Kings 4:39)
41. They went out from us, but they ___ not of us. (1 John 2:19)
43. Beamed light.
45. Southern state.
47. Go ye therefore, and teach all ___. (Matt. 28:19)
51. The ___ of God is according to truth. (Rom. 2:2)
55. He ___ on the ground, and made clay. (John 9:6)
56. Sir, come down ___ my child die. (John 4:49)
57. I saw as it were ___ [2 words] of glass. (Rev. 15:2)
58. But the tongue can no man ___. (James 3:8)
59. Thought to ___ them for himself. (2 Chron. 32:1)
60. I will make thine ___ iron. (Mic. 4:13)
61. Noah begat ___, Ham, and Japheth. (Gen. 5:32)

Down

1. ___ herself received strength to conceive seed. (Heb. 11:11)
2. Mattathias, which was the son of ___, which was the son of Naum. (Luke 3:25)
3. Little children, it is the ___ time. (1 John 2:18)
4. He saw the disciples straining at ___ [2 words]. (Mark 6:48, NIV)
5. The ___ measure that is abominable. (Mic. 6:10)
6. The world by ___ knew not God. (1 Cor. 1:21)
7. Doth the wild ___ bray? (Job 6:5)
8. The city had no ___ of the sun. (Rev. 21:23)
9. Ye have heard of the patience of ___. (James 5:11)
10. Take an ___ and push it through his ear lobe. (Deut. 15:17, NIV)
11. Unit of weight.
17. Their bows will ___ down the young men. (Isa. 13:18, ASV)
19. Whose sandals I am not worthy to ___. (John 1:27, NIV)
22. Until the day that ___ entered into the ark. (Luke 17:27)
24. The twelfth month, that is, the month ___. (Esther 3:7)
25. Draw . . . sin as it were with a cart ___. (Isa . 5:18)

26. The ___ is the word of God. (Luke 8:11)
27. The flame of the fire ___ those men. (Dan. 3:22)
28. We spent our years as a ___ that is told. (Ps. 90:9)
29. Saudi Arabian district.
31. Positive possession.
34. Building wing.
36. For there shall arise false ___. (Matt. 24:24)
39. I speak after the ___ of men. (Rom. 6:19)
42. Is there any taste in the white of an ___? (Job 6:6)

44. I beheld ___ as lightning fall from heaven. (Luke 10:18)
46. Asian nurse.
48. Colorful fish.
49. His ___ is called The Word of God. (Rev. 19:13)
50. There shall come forth a rod out of the ___ of Jesse. (Isa. 11:1)
51. Take hold of the skirt of him that is a ___. (Zech. 8:23)
52. Tell site.
53. Ye have made it a ___ of thieves. (Mark 11:17)
54. Inner (comb. form).

12

Across

1. Hebrew word for house.
5. This woman was taken in adultery, in the very ___. (John 8:4)
8. Equestrian command.
12. Swiss river.
13. Through prefix.
14. ___, ye; for the day of the LORD is at hand. (Isa. 13:6)
15. Caesar (Russian).
16. Believed not that he was a ___. (Acts 9:26)
18. The ___ hope shall perish. (Job. 8:13)
20. I will give thee rain in ___ season. (Lev. 26:4)
21. He ___ his money; for, behold, it was in his sack's mouth. (Gen. 42:27)
25. A colt the foal of an ___. (Matt. 21:5)
28. Shush sound.
30. Automation prefix.
31. Scottish shipyards.
33. He cometh with clouds; and every eye shall ___ him. (Rev. 1:7)
35. Were as swift as ___ upon the mountains. (1 Chron. 12:8)
36. Then shall the ___ of the wood sing. (1 Chron. 16:33)
38. I ___ the pride of Judah. (Jer. 13:9)
40. Direction: Jerusalem to Tiberias [75 miles].
41. Isaac brought her into his mother ___ tent. (Gen. 24:67)
43. The name of the wicked shall ___. (Prov. 10:7)
45. Ye build the ___ of the prophets. (Luke 11:47)
50. He behaveth himself ___ toward his virgin. (1 Cor. 7:36)
53. Ancient letter.
54. How ___ is the fig tree withered. (Matt. 21:20)
55. ___, lama sabachthani? (Matt. 27:46)

56. There is a bad ___, for he has been there four days. (John 11:39, NIV)
57. He who makes haste with his feet ___. (Prov. 19:2, ASV)
58. Say, Thy God, O ___, liveth. (Amos 8:14)
59. Ye see a cloud rise out of the ___. (Luke 12:54)

Down

1. Ten acres of vineyard shall yield one ___. (Isa. 5:10)
2. Knowledge is ___ unto him that understandeth. (Prov. 14:6)
3. Let their table be a snare, and a ___. (Rom. 11:9)
4. ___ said, John have I beheaded. (Luke 9:9)
5. I could not ___ you as spiritual. (1 Cor. 3:1, NIV)
6. 103 (Roman numerals).
7. O ___ and see that the LORD is good. (Ps. 34:8)
8. All that hate me ___ together. (Ps. 41:7)
9. All winged insects are unclean, except those that ___, (Lev. 11:21, GNB)
10. I am like an ___ of the desert. (Ps. 102:6)
11. Bitter beer.
17. Luck of the Irish.
19. Three shepherds also I ___ off. (Zech. 11:8)
22. I will make your heaven as ___. (Lev. 26:19)
23. Are not ___ ye in the presence of our Lord Jesus Christ? (1 Thess. 2:19)
24. A portion of the whole.
25. Many of them which also used curious ___. (Acts 19:19)
26. ___ obeyed Abraham, calling him lord. (1 Peter 3:6)

27. O thou ___, go, flee thee away. (Amos 7:12)
29. Egyptian sun god.
32. He changeth the times and the ___. (Dan. 2:21)
34. They entered into the temple ___ [2 words] the morning. (Acts 5:21)
37. The sons of ___; Elam, and Asshur. (1 Chron. 1:17)
39. Mythological bird.
42. Neither bid him God ___. (2 John 10)
44. They shall build, but I will ___ down (Mal. 1:4)

46. The sons of ___; Arah, and Haniel. (1 Chron. 7:39)
47. Though I be ___ in speech. (2 Cor. 11:6)
48. The days of ___ were nine hundred and five years. (Gen. 5:11)
49. Spanish painter.
50. When ye pray, ___ not vain repetitions. (Matt. 6:7)
51. ___ yet that he should offer himself often. (Heb. 9:25)
52. Ye shall offer the tenth part of a bath out of the ___. (Ezek. 45:14)

13

Across

1. Whose truth shall be a spider's ___. (Job 8:14)
4. I, even I, will ___ unto the Lord. (Judg. 5:3)
8. He will be like a refiner's fire or a launderer's ___. (Mal. 3:2, NIV)
12. Have (Scottish).
13. John had his raiment of camel's ___. (Matt. 3:4)
14. Literary leaf.
15. Out of whose womb came the ____? (Job 38:29)
16. Woe to them that . . . sin as it were with a cart ___. (Isa. 5:18)
17. He shall rule them with a rod of ___. (Rev. 19:15)
18. Friend, lend me ___ loaves. (Luke 11:5)
20. Scorch.
22. Stand in ___, and sin not. (Ps. 4:4)
24. He ___, 'No eye will see me.' (Job 24:15, NIV)
28. I saw the ___ pushing westward. (Dan. 8:4)
31. Thou shalt not take the ___ with the young. (Deut. 22:6)
33. To put an end to sin, to ___ for wickedness. (Dan. 9:24, NIV)
34. They are like grass which sprouts ___. (Ps. 90:5, ASV)
36. Philip ___ thither to him. (Acts 8:30)
38. He saith to the ___, Be thou on the earth. (Job 37:6)
39. Let him that stole ___ no more. (Eph. 4:28)
41. Cast out the bondwoman and ___ son. (Gal. 4:30)
43. God created man in his ___ image. (Gen. 1:27)
44. Thou hast had a perpetual ___. (Ezek. 35:5)
46. Who verily ___ foreordained before the foundation of the world. (1 Peter 1:20)
48. My God shall supply all your ___. (Phil. 4:19)
50. By these were the ___ of the Gentiles divided in their lands. (Gen. 10:5)
54. ___, the Ahohite. (1 Chron. 11:29)
57. When he ___ his arrows, let them be as headless shafts. (Ps. 58:7, ASV)
59. Beloved, let us love ___ another. (1 John 4:7)
60. The unclean spirit had ___ him. (John 1:26)
61. Every ___ is known by his own fruit. (Luke 6:44)
62. This is my beloved ___, in whom I am well pleased. (2 Peter 1:17)
63. My lover is like a gazelle or a young ___. (Song of Sol. 2:9, NIV)
64. The men that ___ Jesus mocked him. (Luke 22:63)
65. Superlative ending.

Down

1. Samuel told him every ___. (1 Sam. 3:18)
2. Let ___ esteem other better than themselves. (Phil. 2:3)
3. Jotham ran away, and fled, and went to ___. (Judg. 9:21)
4. Therefore be as ___ as snakes. (Matt. 10:16, NIV)
5. Wattlebird.
6. Little bites.
7. ___ one another with an holy kiss. (2 Cor. 13:12)
8. Try the ___ whether they are of God. (1 John 4:1)
9. All that handle the ___, the mariners. (Ezek. 27:29)
10. They would have repented long ___. (Matt. 11:21)
11. My tongue is the ___ of a ready writer. (Ps. 45:1)
19. Economic adviser.
21. ___, I am warm, I have seen the fire. (Isa. 44:16)
23. He that hath an ___, let him hear. (Rev. 2:11)

25. Italian ninth.
26. I ___ their imagination. (Deut. 31:21)
27. I have ___ sackcloth over my skin. (Job. 16:15, NKJ)
28. The ___ shall understand knowledge. (Isa. 32:4)
29. Projection of Greek temple.
30. I will make him an help ___ for him. (Gen. 2:18)
32. Mahagony (abbr.).
35. To whom shall I speak, and give ___? (Jer. 6:10)
37. I will write upon him my ___ name. (Rev. 3:12)
40. We sailed to the ___ of Crete. (Acts 27:7, NIV)
42. God hath ___ him from the dead. (Rom. 10:9)

45. There is a sin unto ___. (1 John 5:16)
47. Infield position.
49. A ___ vision was shown to me. (Isa. 21:2, NIV)
51. He that loveth his life shall ___ it. (John 12:25)
52. Seth lived after he begat ___ 807 years. (Gen. 5:7)
53. The Father ___ the Son to be the Saviour. (1 John 4:14)
54. That which groweth of ___ own accord. (Lev. 25:5)
55. The ___ fell upon Matthias. (Acts 1:26)
56. Jephunneh, and Pispah, and ___. (1 Chron. 7:38)
58. Honey.

14

Across

1. Shall be astonished, and ___ his head. (Jer. 18:16)
4. Dwelt in Michmash, and ___, and Bethel. (Neh. 11:31)
8. And he was strong as the ___. (Amos 2:9)
12. ___ the son of Ikkesh the Tekoite. (2 Sam. 23:26)
13. He shall pluck away his ___ with his feathers. (Lev. 1:16)
14. The body is a ___. (1 Cor. 12:12, NIV)
15. Jonah rose up to flee unto ___. (Jonah 1:3)
17. We spend our years as a ___ that is told. (Ps. 90:9)
18. ___ went forth conquering, and to conquer. (Rev. 6:2)
19. They presumed to go up unto the ___ [2 words]. (Num. 14:44)
21. Then shall ye bring down my ___ hairs with sorrow to the grave. (Gen. 42:38)
24. We went into the province of ___. (Ezra 5:8)
25. To make ill.
26. Feathered scarf.
27. Positive possession.
31. Contemptibly small.
33. Hadassah, that is, ___.
34. ___ had waited till Job had spoken. (Job. 32:4)
35. I ___ on the judgment seat. (Acts 25:17)
36. The children of Lod, Hadid, and ___. (Neh. 7:37)
37. Acid reaction fragrance.
39. Do not ___ the LORD your God. (Deut. 6:16, NIV)
40. The king's chamberlains, ___ and Teresh. (Esther 2:21)
43. They fled before the men of ___. (Josh. 7:4)
44. ___ bare to Esau Eliphaz. (Gen. 36:4)
45. Esther did the commandment of ___. (Esther 2:10)
50. High (Latin).
51. He entered the temple ___. (Luke 19:45, NIV)
52. Bow-like.
53. Malicious look.
54. He gave them hail for ___. (Ps. 105:32)
55. The ___ that is in the land of Assyria. (Isa. 7:18)

Down

1. We do you to ___ of the grace of God. (2 Cor. 8:1)
2. Jephunneh, and Pispah, and ___. (1 Chron. 7:38)
3. Needlefish.
4. Even in laughter the heart may ___. (Prov. 14:13, NIV)
5. Ussi and Ussiel, and Jerimoth, and ___. (1 Chron. 7:7)
6. Now ___ was clothed with filthy garments. (Zech. 3:3)
7. Sap sucking insect.
8. To endure longer.
9. Assyrian sun god.
10. 1000 (comb. form).
11. There is but a ___ between me and death. (1 Sam. 20:3)
16. He does not ___ away from the sword. (Job 39:22, NIV)
20. Set them to judge who are ___ esteemed. (1 Cor. 6:4)
21. The lazy man does not roast his ___. (Prov. 12:27, NIV)
22. Canadian insurgent.
23. Russian mountain range.
24. The babe leaped in my womb for ___. (Luke 1:44)
26. I am ashamed and ___ to lift up my face. (Ezra 9:6)
28. The house of him that hath his ___ loosed. (Deut. 25:10)
29. Poetical odd's opposite.

30. Jog pace.
32. One of Ahasuerus' (Xerxes') advisors. (Esther 1:14)
33. Give ___, O LORD, unto my prayer. (Ps. 86:6)
35. Spanish madam.
38. So ___ remained desolate in her brother Absalom's house. (2 Sam. 13:20)
39. Bind them continually upon thine heart, and ___ them about thy neck. (Prov. 6:21)
40. Ahab served ___ a little. (2 Kings 10:18)
41. Withal they learn to be ___. (1 Tim. 5:13)
42. Enter ye in at the strait ___. (Matt. 7:13)
43. King of Babylon gave charge concerning Jeremiah to Nebuzar-___. (Jer. 39:11)
46. Shemei and ___, and the mighty men which belonged to David. (1 Kings 1:8)
47. The fourth part of a ___ of dove's dung. (2 Kings 6:25)
48. Remember them that ___ in bonds. (Heb. 13:3)
49. Out of whose womb came the ___? (Job 38:29)

15

Across

1. Love worketh no ___ to his neighbour. (Rom. 13:10)
4. ___ told Jezebel all that Elijah had done. (1 Kings 19:1)
8. Asian nurse.
12. ___ that none render evil for evil. (1 Thess. 5:15)
13. The harvest of the earth is ___. (Rev. 14:15)
14. Doth God take ___ for oxen? (1 Cor. 9:9)
15. ___ hospitality one to another. (1 Peter 4:9)
16. Drained of substance.
17. [Mary] wiped his feet with her ___. (John 12:3)
18. Done unto . . . the Egyptians for ___ sake. (Exod. 18:8)
20. Red gems.
21. A ___ tongue brings angry looks. (Prov. 25:23, NIV)
22. Number in Roman trinity.
23. Send men to ___ and call for Simon. (Acts 11:13)
26. ___ fell upon his face, and laughed. (Gen. 17:17)
30. Thy Urim be with thy holy ___. (Deut. 33:8)
31. Theatre sign.
32. ___, the valley of craftsmen. (Neh. 11:35)
33. Ye men of ___, why stand ye gazing up? (Acts 1:11)
36. Bless them that ___ you. (Luke 6:28)
38. The ___ that was washed to her wallowing. (2 Peter 2:22)
39. To his [Cain] offering he ___ not respect. (Gen. 4:5)
40. Who will ___ the battle? (1 Kings 20:14, NIV)
43. Stand upon mount ___ to bless the people. (Deut. 27:12)
47. Brought them unto Halah, and Hasbor, and ___. (1 Chron. 5:26)

48. ___ begat Aminadab. (Matt. 1:4)
49. ___ the son of Ikkesh the Tekoite. (2 Sam. 23:26)
50. To the sheltered side.
51. These ___ power to shut heaven. (Rev. 11:6)
52. Achar, who brought disaster on Israel by violating the ___ on taking devoted things. (1 Chron. 2:7, NIV)
53. Take the millstones, and grind ___. (Isa. 47:2)
54. The LORD had respect unto ___. (Gen. 4:4)
55. Neither shall ___ Priest drink wine. (Ezek. 44:21)

Down

1. The sons of Asher: Jimnah, and Ishuah, and ___ (Gen. 46:17)
2. How much ___ man, that is a worm? (Job:25:6)
3. To ogle.
4. City E. of Nineveh.
5. The inhabitants of Megiddo and its towns—three ___ regions. (Josh. 17:11, NKJV)
6. Bringing gold, and silver, ivory, and ___, and peacocks. (1 Kings 10:22)
7. If I make my ___ in hell, behold, thou art there. (Ps. 139:8)
8. Gallio was the deputy of ___. (Acts 18:12)
9. Volcanic crater.
10. It goes through ___ places seeking rest. (Luke 11:24, NIV)
11. If the firstborn son be ___ that was hated. (Deut. 21:15)
19. The child shall play on the hole of an ___. (Isa. 11:8)
20. Saying, ___, we would see Jesus. (John 12:21)
22. Nigerian tribe.
23. Trotter's pace.
24. Cape Horn native.
25. Clay.

26. Ye ___ clean, but not all. (John 13:10)
27. As Aaron thy brother died in mount ___. (Deut. 32:50)
28. Autograph note signed.
29. Man's nickname.
31. A time to rend, and a time to ___. (Eccles. 3:7)
34. Shall be called no more Jacob, but ___. (Gen. 32:28)
35. The ___ fell upon Matthias. (Acts 1:26)
36. Elijah went up to the top of ___. (1 Kings 18:42)
37. Caucasian language.
39. The wave breast and ___ shoulder shall ye eat in a clean place. (Lev. 10:14)

40. Counterfeit.
41. The ___ of bricks . . . ye shall lay upon them. (Exod. 5:8)
42. Children shouting in the temple ___. (Matt. 21:15, NIV)
43. Seven women will ___ hold of one man. (Isa. 4:1, GNB)
44. The king said unto him, Art thou ___? (2 Sam. 9:2)
45. Formerly Persia.
46. His voice as the sound of ___ waters. (Rev. 1:15)
48. ___, she is broken that was the gates of the people. (Ezek. 26:2)

16

Across

1. They cast Pur, that is, the ___.
   (Esther 3:7)
4. Israel journeyed, and spread his tent beyond the tower of ___. (Gen. 35:21)
8. Thus ___ saith, Jeroboam shall die. (Amos 7:11)
12. Hear this, ye old men, and give ___.
   (Joel 1:2)
13. Smooth sound.
14. Hereditary unit.
15. Sir, come down ___ my child die.
   (John 4:49)
16. Religious image.
17. The ___ is not to the swift. (Eccles. 9:11)
18. Five chapter N.T. book.
21. Joash was minded to ___ the house.
   (2 Chron. 24:4)
23. We shall all be changed, in a moment, in the twinkling of an ___.
   (1 Cor. 15:52)
24. Woe to those who ___ evil statues.
   (Isa. 10:1, ASV)
25. Town prefix.
26. I was ___ and afraid to tell you. (Job 32:6, ASV)
29. Meaningless talk.
30. Distress signal.
31. They break their bones, and ___ them in pieces. (Mic. 3:3)
32. The dumb ___ speaking with man's voice. (2 Peter 2:16)
33. The trees of the LORD are full of ___.
   (Ps. 104:16)
34. ___ said, Turn again, my daughters.
   (Ruth 1:11)
35. Her ___ is to be devoted to the Lord.
   (1 Cor. 7:34, NIV)
36. The child ___ ministered unto the LORD. (1 Sam. 3:1)
37. Thirty-one chapter O.T. book.
41. ___ bare to Esau Eliphaz. (Gen. 36:4)

42. Few (comb. form).
43. The ___ sitting upon the young.
   (Deut. 22:6)
46. To let or leave (obs.).
47. Taurus star.
48. Direction: Bethlehem to Jerusalem [10 kms.].
49. Young girl.
50. Printer's direction.
51. And ___ greedily after the error of Balaam. (Jude 11)

Down

1. We sailed to the ___ of Crete. (Acts 27:7, NIV)
2. All that handle the ___, the mariners. (Ezek. 27:29)
3. What is my ___? what is my sin?
   (Gen. 31:36)
4. To bring to light.
5. Decorative style.
6. He that heareth the word, and ___ with joy receiveth it. (Matt. 13:20)
7. See that no one ___ evil for evil. (1 Thess. 5:15, NKJ)
8. ___ with thine adversary quickly.
   (Matt. 5:25)
9. His young ones cry unto God, they wander for lack of ___. (Job 38:41)
10. It is appointed unto men ___ to die, but after this the judgment. (Heb. 9:27)
11. A Prophet was beforetime called a ___. (1 Sam. 9:9)
19. In the habitation of dragons, where ___ lay. (Isa. 35:7)
20. Engraver.
21. Zur, and Hur, and ___, which were dukes. (Josh. 13:21)
22. ___ lived ninety years, and begat Cainan. (Gen. 5:9)
25. A tower, whose ___ may reach unto heaven. (Gen. 11:4)
26. Gave it unto Hagar, putting it on her ___. (Gen. 21:14)

27. Learn first to shew piety at ___. (1 Tim. 5:4)
28. Philippine tree.
30. They said unto ___ wife, Entice thy husband. (Judg. 14:15)
31. Great Babylon ___ in remembrance before God. (Rev. 16:19)
33. ___ thou here in a good place. (James 2:3)
34. The water is ___, and the ground barren. (2 Kings 2:19)
35. I am become like dust and ___. (Job 30:19)

36. ___ a scorner, and the simple will beware. (Prov. 19:25)
37. They stumbled that they should ___. (Rom. 11:11)
38. "Is that your own ___," Jesus asked. (John 18:34, NIV)
39. The chest containing the gold ___ and the models of tumors. (1 Sam. 6:11, NIV)
40. Salted.
44. Literary selections.
45. The sons of God saw the daughters of ___ that they were fair. (Gen. 6:2)

17

Across

1. Let us search and ___ our ways. (Lam. 3:40)
4. Whosoever shall say to his brother, ___, shall be in danger. (Matt. 5:22)
8. Agile.
12. As for all the hills once cultivated by the ___. (Isa. 7:25, NIV)
13. The son of ___ made a conspiracy. (2 Kings 15:30)
14. There is one come out of ___ that imagineth evil against the LORD. (Nah. 1:11)
15. Largest federalist republic.
16. Call me not Naomi, call me ___. (Ruth 1:20)
17. Disencumbers.
18. O LORD, truly I am thy ___. (Ps. 116:16)
20. Formal dance (French).
21. Earth.
22. My ___ boiled, and rested not. (Job 30:27)
25. As for the ___, the fir trees are her house. (Ps. 104:17)
28. ___, Repent: for the kingdom of heaven is at hand. (Matt. 4:17)
29. Their bows will ___ down the young men. (Isa. 13:18, ASV)
30. The people below look as ___ as ants. (Isa. 40:22, GNB)
31. ___ shall be a serpent by the way. (Gen. 49:17)
32. Property (Latin).
33. Ye all ___ partakers of my grace. (Phil. 1:7)
34. Let me ___, and let another eat. (Job 31:8)
35. It was in my mouth sweet as ___. (Rev. 10:10)
36. Thou shalt have none to ___ them. (Deut. 28:31)
38. Sludge.
39. Charged atom.
40. He who loveth God, love his ___ also. (1 John 4:21)
44. Vapor (comb. form).

46. Slew of the Philistines six hundred men with an ox ___. (Judg. 3:31)
47. Adam was first formed, then ___. (1 Tim. 2:13)
48. At midnight ___ and Silas prayed. (Acts 16:25)
49. In that he died, he died unto sin ___. (Rom. 6:10)
50. Hath Satan filled thine heart to ___? (Acts 5:3)
51. Hardy heroine.
52. What ___ is this that ye have done? (Gen. 44:15)
53. The ___ favoured and leanfleshed kine. (Gen. 41:4)

Down

1. ___ Esau despised his birthright. (Gen. 25:34)
2. Christ both died, and ___, and revived. (Rom. 14:9)
3. Preach the acceptable ___ of the Lord. (Luke 4:19)
4. At this ___, Moses fled. (Acts 7:29, ASV)
5. ___ [2 words] of bread and vineyards. (Isa. 36:17)
6. Uzza and Ahio drave the ___. (1 Chron. 13:7)
7. ___, even the ancient high places are ours. (Ezek. 36:2)
8. The lion shall eat ___ like the bullock. (Isa. 65:25)
9. Unto ___ our dearly beloved. (Philem. 1)
10. It will be foul weather today; for the sky is ___ and lowring. (Matt. 16:3)
11. ___, Lord, yet the dogs under the table eat. (Mark 7:28)
19. Your zeal hath provoked ___ many. (2 Cor. 9:2)
20. And have given a ___ for an harlot. (Joel 3:3)
22. Achar, who brought disaster on Israel by violating the ___. (1 Chron. 2:7, NIV)

23. Seeing a ___ fig tree by the road. (Matt. 21:19, ASV)
24. On the tops of the hills may it ___. (Ps. 72:16, NIV)
25. Your images, the ___ of your god. (Amos 5:26)
26. Bind the ___ of thine head. (Ezek. 24:17)
27. ___, whom I have begotten in my bonds. (Philem. 10)
28. I ___ three unclean spirits like frogs. (Rev. 16:13)
31. Do you watch when the ___ bears her fawn? (Job 39:1, NIV)
32. Every warrior's ___ used in battle. (Isa. 9:5, NIV)
34. There is one glory of the ___. (1 Cor. 15:41)
35. Having one's head covered.
37. As a cloud ___ a hot day. (Isa. 25:5, GNB)
38. If by ___, then is it no more of works. (Rom. 11:6)
40. A ___ of his shall not be broken. (John 19:36)
41. Joseph, which was the son of ___. (Luke 3:23)
42. Thou canst not bear them which are ___. (Rev. 2:2)
43. They ___ to and fro, and stagger. (Ps. 107:27)
44. All that were strong and ___ for war. (2 Kings 24:16)
45. Toe (Scottish).
46. ___ shall wipe away all tears. (Rev. 21:4)

18

Across

1. One goeth with a ___ to come into the mountain of the Lord. (Isa. 30:29)
5. With lies ye have made the heart of the righteous ___. (Ezek. 13:22)
8. Death rattle.
12. ___ for the day! for the day of the Lord is at hand. (Joel 1:15)
13. Their lies caused them to ___. (Amos 2:4)
14. Bullfight cheers.
15. Hath God ___ away his people? (Rom. 11:1)
16. ___ the kine to the cart. (1 Sam. 6:7)
17. The bud shall yield no ___. (Hos. 8:7)
18. Ye ___ mint and rue and all manner of herbs. (Luke 11:42)
20. The burden of the word of the Lord to Israel by ___. (Mal. 1:1)
22. Time period.
24. The tabernacle of God is with ___. (Rev. 2:3)
25. Simon Peter is whose brother?
29. The sons of ___ his brother were, Ulam his firstborn, Jehush the second, and Eliphelet. (1 Chron. 8:39)
33. River rapids (French).
34. Take, ___; this is my body. (1 Cor. 11:24)
36. Panay native.
37. The daughter of Asher was ___. (Num. 26:46)
40. Those virgins arose, and ___ their lamps. (Matt. 25:7)
43. Fly larva.
45. They feast with ___, feeding themselves. (Jude 12)
46. The ___ came forth out of the holes. (1 Sam. 14:11)
50. Deborah: awake, awake, ___ a song. (Judg. 5:12)
54. ___ the scribe stood upon a pulpit of wood. (Neh. 8:4)
55. There was no room for them in the ___. (Luke 2:7)
57. There came forth two she bears out of the wood, and ___ forty and two children of them. (2 Kings 2:24)
58. Five hundred sheets.
59. Wooden pail.
60. The iniquity of ___ house shall not be purged. (1 Sam. 3:14)
61. Many of them also which used curious ___ brought their books together. (Acts 19:19)
62. Lord, behold, here are ___ swords. (Luke 22:38)
63. The earth did quake, and the rocks ___. (Matt. 27:51)

Down

1. You made a ___ with those whose beds you love. (Isa. 57:8, NIV)
2. ___ the Ahohite. (1 Chron. 11:29)
3. The remission of sins that are ___. (Rom. 3:25)
4. He brought up Hadassah, that is, ___. (Esther 2:7)
5. I have ___ before thee an open door. (Rev. 3:8)
6. The children of Kirjath-___, Chephirah and Beeroth. (Ezra 2:25)
7. I have suffered many things this day in a ___ because of him. (Matt. 27:19)
8. They have beaten us openly uncondemned, being ___. (Acts 16:37)
9. Small fish.
10. ___ was tender eyed. (Gen. 29:17)
11. Naum, which was the son of ___. (Luke 3:25)
19. How long will it be ___ ye make an end. (Job 18:2)
21. We sailed to the ___ of Crete. (Acts 27:7)
23. Stand in ___, and sin not. (Ps. 4:4)
25. Jesse took an ___ laden with bread. (1 Sam. 16:20)

1	2	3	4		5	6	7		8	9	10	11
12					13				14			
15					16				17			
18				19		20		21				
			22		23		24					
25	26	27				28		29		30	31	32
33					34		35			36		
37			38	39		40		41	42			
			43		44		45					
46	47	48				49		50		51	52	53
54					55		56			57		
58					59				60			
61					62				63			

26. Free from taboo.
27. The son of Abinadab, in all the region of ___. (1 Kings 4:11)
28. I have not ___ with vain persons. (Ps. 26:4)
30. Jacob sojourned in the land of ___. (Ps. 105:23)
31. Summer in Paris (Fr.).
32. Yet thou never gavest me a ___. (Luke 15:29)
35. To ___ them that dwell upon the earth. (Rev. 3:10)
38. They took Lot, ___ brother's son. (Gen. 14:12)
39. Any hill which could be dug with the ___. (Isa. 7:25, NKJ)
41. Debt note.

42. Unto wizards that peep, and that ___. (Isa. 8:19)
44. All day long they ___ my words. (Ps. 56:5)
46. Goddess queen.
47. The sons of ___, Bilhan, and Zavan. (1 Chron. 1:42)
48. I know what a cocky ___ you are. (1 Sam. 17:28, LB)
49. Her Nazarites were purer than ___. (Lam. 4:7)
51. We spend our years as a ___ that is told. (Ps. 90:9)
52. Ireland.
53. Ye shall find ___ unto your souls. (Matt. 11:29)
56. New (comb. form.).

19

Across

1. His mother's name also was ___. (2 Kings 18:2)
4. Walk component.
8. That which was spoken by the prophet ___. (Acts 2:16)
12. I ___ no rest in my spirit. (2 Cor. 2:13)
13. Unto us a child is born, unto us ___ [2 words] is given. (Isa. 9:6)
14. Repent; or ___ I will come unto thee. (Rev. 2:16)
15. ___ Israel will be saved. (Rom. 11:26)
16. ___ thee with badgers' skin. (Ezek. 16:10)
17. Heaven is like to a grain of mustard ___. (Matt. 13:31)
18. If a man loudly ___ his neighbor early in the morning, it will be taken as a curse. (Prov. 27:14, NIV)
20. "Et ___, Brute! Then fall, Caesar!"
21. Even as a ___ gathereth her chickens. (Matt. 23:37)
22. The burden of the ___ of the sea. (Isa. 21:1)
26. They ___ bitter speech as their arrow. (Ps. 64:3, ASV)
29. If thou doest not well, ___ lieth at the door. (Gen. 4:7)
30. Deliver thyself as a ___ from the hand of the hunter. (Prov. 6:5)
31. I will ___ water for thy camels, also. (Gen. 24:19)
32. The priest shall take some of the ___ of oil. (Lev. 14:15)
33. For this ___ is mount Sinai. (Gal. 4:25)
34. He touched his ___, and healed him. (Luke 22:51)
35. Woe to the women that ___ pillows. (Ezek. 13:18)
36. There was given to me a ___ in the flesh. (2 Cor. 12:7)
37. Thou shalt have none to ___ them. (Deut. 28:31)
39. He that will love life, and ___ good days. (1 Peter 3:10)
40. ___ hath chosen us in him before the foundation of the world. (Eph. 1:4)
41. ___ this stone that it be made bread. (Luke 4:3)
45. Even in laughter the heart may ___. (Prov. 14:13, NIV)
48. Is not my ___ in me? and is wisdom driven quite from me? (Job 6:13)
49. Images of your mice that ___ the land. (1 Sam. 6:5)
50. A man plucked off his ___, and gave it to his neighbour. (Ruth 4:7)
51. To encourage.
52. Wine vessel.
53. O thou ___, go, flee thee away into the land of Judah. (Amos 7:12)
54. Swords flashing, spears gleaming, many slain, a ___ of corpses. (Nah. 3:3, ASV)
55. Make bare the ___, uncover the thigh, pass over the waters. (Isa. 47:2)

Down

1. ___ said to Elijah, Hast thou found me. (1 Kings 21:20)
2. Toss thee like a ___ into a large country. (Isa. 22:18)
3. They be ___, therefore they cry. (Exod. 5:8)
4. We have ___ from death unto life. (1 John 3:14)
5. I looked, and behold, an ___ horse. (Rev. 6:8, ASV)
6. We came with a straight course unto ___. (Acts 21:1)
7. Whose ___ is destruction, whose God is their belly. (Phil. 3:19)
8. Then said ___, Father, forgive them. (Luke 23:34)
9. Oil suffix.
10. Direction: Jerusalem to Masada [34 miles].
11. I have ___ thee in right paths. (Prov. 4:11)
19. Study to ___ thyself approved unto God. (2 Tim. 2:15)
20. Let Haman's ___ sons be hanged. (Esther 9:13)

22. Though they ___ into hell. (Amos 9:2)

23. Therefore.

24. We ___ all like bears, and mourn sore like doves (Isa. 59:11)

25. Shore bird.

26. Zebadiah, and Arad, and ___. (1 Chron. 8:15)

27. "Dies ___," the 'Day of Wrath.'

28. Paul stood in the midst of ___ hill. (Acts 17:22)

29. In the morning ___ thy seed. (Eccles. 11:6)

32. We sailed to the ___ of Crete. (Acts 27:7, NIV)

33. Catching sound.

35. If any man will ___ thee at the law. (Matt. 5:40)

36. God cannot be tempted by evil, and he himself ___ no one. (James 1:13, GNB)

38. He shall be free at home one year, and shall ___ up his wife. (Deut. 24:5)

39. They shall be ashes under the ___ of your feet. (Mal. 4:3)

41. Tropical tree.

42. Zophah, and Imna, and Shelesh, and ___. (1 Chron. 7:35)

43. His ___ is called The Word of God. (Rev. 19:13)

44. They sacrifice unto their net, and burn incense unto their ___. (Hab. 1:16)

45. Issachar is a strong ___ couching down. (Gen. 49:14)

46. Asian shrub.

47. The hills once cultivated by the ___. (Isa. 7:25, NIV)

48. Jacob sojourned in the land of ___. (Ps. 105:23)

41

20

Across

1. She got a papyrus basket for him and coated it with ___ and pitch. (Exod. 2:3, NIV)
4. Where is the ___ of your mother's divorcement? (Isa. 50:1)
8. There was a marriage in ___ of Galilee. (John 2:1)
12. Even to your old ___, I am he. (Isa. 46:4)
13. I will go with you; if he is in the ___, I will track him down. (1 Sam. 23:23, NIV)
14. The sons of Dishan; Uz and ___. (1 Chron. 1:42)
15. ___ Fail, Irish stone.
16. Iru, Elah, and ___: the sons of Elah. (1 Chron. 4:15)
17. Covet earnestly the ___ gifts. (1 Cor. 12:31)
18. Erastus abode at ___. (2 Tim. 4:20)
20. Ra son.
21. Sheepfold.
22. Every one shall be ___ with fire. (Mark 9:49)
26. ___, arrayed in royal apparel, sat upon his throne, and made an oration. (Acts 12:21)
29. Be gentle unto all men, ___ to teach. (2 Tim. 2:24)
30. Why make you this ___, and weep? (Mark 5:39)
31. The high places also of ___, the sin of Israel, shall be destroyed. (Hos. 10:8)
32. Who can withstand his ___ blast? (Ps. 147:17, NIV)
33. Jesus Christ be with you all. ___. (Rev. 22:21)
34. The ___, which the LORD God had taken from man, made he woman. (Gen. 2:22)
35. I took the little book out of the angel's hand, and ___ it up. (Rev. 10:10)
36. The night is far ___, the day is at hand. (Rom. 13:12)
37. Warnings of danger.
39. When ___ thousand years are expired, Satan shall be loosed out of his prison. (Rev. 20:7)
40. Howl, O Hesbon, for ___ is spoiled (Jer. 49:3)
41. Deliver us from this ___ evil world. (Gal. 1:4)
45. Related by blood.
48. ___ to yourselves, that we lose not those things which we have wrought. (2 John 8)
49. Naphtali is a ___ set free. (Gen. 49:21, NIV)
50. Paul and Silas prayed, and ___ praises. (Acts 16:25)
51. Feminine French pronoun.
52. Annam measure.
53. Ye shall ___ away for your iniquities. (Ezek. 24:23)
54. I will ___ thee the mystery of the woman. (Rev. 17:7)
55. I begin, I will also make an ___. (1 Sam. 3:12)

Down

1. Fine-grained mineral.
2. Money exchange fee.
3. Go up, ___ an altar unto the Lord. (2 Sam. 24:18)
4. Abhor it, for it is something ___. (Deut. 7:26, ASV)
5. Enraged.
6. ___ said, A troop cometh; and she called his name Gad. (Gen. 30:11)
7. Five chapter O.T. book abbreviation.
8. And goeth out to ___ on the left hand. (Josh. 19:27)
9. Unto the pure all things ___ pure. (Titus 1:15)
10. Of the nose (Latin).
11. Go to the ___, thou sluggard. (Prov. 6:6)
19. Cast it in thither; and the ___ did swim. (2 Kings 6:6)
20. I ___ on the judgment seat. (Acts 25:17)
22. Go and ___ where he is, that I may send and fetch him. (2 Kings 6:13)
23. The tongue can no man ___. (James 3:8)
24. The land is as the garden of ___ before them. (Joel 2:3)

25. Jesus sent him home, saying, ___ go into the village. (Mark 8:26, NIV)

26. Unto Halah, and Habor, and ___. (1 Chron. 5:26)

27. Thou canst not bear them which are ___. (Rev. 2:2)

28. Zur, and Hur, and ___ which were dukes. (Josh. 13:21)

29. One spot or one shot.

32. That which groweth of ___ own accord of thy harvest thou shalt not reap. (Lev. 25:5)

33. Came the navy of Tharshish bringing gold, and silver, ivory, and ___, and peacocks. (1 Kings 10:22)

35. Pochereth of Zegaim, the children of ___. (Ezra 2:57)

36. Making the ephah small, and the ___ great. (Amos 8:5)

38. The ___ of mountains is his pasture. (Job 39:8)

39. To sing heartily.

41. Make thee a fiery serpent, and set it upon a ___. (Num. 21:8)

42. The children's teeth are set on ___. (Ezek. 18:2)

43. I will cause the sun to go down at ___. (Amos 8:9)

44. The diligent ___ only to plenteousness. (Prov. 21:5)

45. The sucking child shall play on the hold of the ___. (Isa. 11:8)

46. Island food.

47. By the way in the ___, that the Lord met him, and sought to kill him. (Exod. 4:24)

48. ___ us not rend it, but cast lots for it. (John 19:24)

21

Across

1. Jesus began to preach, and to ___, Repent. (Matt. 4:17)
4. Heman, a singer, the son of ___. (1 Chron. 6:33)
8. Moistens.
12. Direction: Cana to Tiberians [20 kms.].
13. East London dwelling.
14. American-Canadian lake.
15. Afternoon social.
16. Let him ___ your left cheek too. (Matt. 5:39, GNB)
17. He has brought Greeks into the temple ___. (Acts 21:28, NIV)
18. Thou shalt not call her name Sarai, but ___. (Gen. 17:15)
20. Wilt thou ___ it up in three days? (John 2:20)
22. If any man will ___ thee at the law. (Matt. 5:40)
24. God, who ___ the dead. (2 Cor. 1:9, NIV)
28. Evil's prefix.
31. Go to the ___, thou sluggard. (Prov. 6:6)
33. Er, the father of ___. (1 Chron. 4:21)
34. They sung as it were ___ [2 words] song. (Rev. 14:3)
36. Son of man, ___ now in the wall. (Ezek. 8:8)
38. Lord, ___ us: we perish. (Matt. 8:25)
39. Polite.
41. Pouchlike structure.
43. The ___ is shorter than that a man can stretch. (Isa. 28:20)
44. The Lord ___ the nations who do not go up to celebrate the Feast of Booths. (Zech. 14:18, ASV)
46. Destroy him that had ___ power of death. (Heb. 2:14)
48. Daughter (Lat.).
50. He was ___ in a cloud, with a rainbow. (Rev. 10:1, NIV)
54. She gave me of the ___, and I did eat. (Gen. 3:12)
57. ___ the Ahohite. (1 Chron. 11:29)
59. Adam was first formed, then ___. (1 Tim. 2:13)
60. Fine ___ have been poured upon me. (Ps. 92:10, NIV)
61. He shall pay for the ___ of his time. (Exod. 21:19)
62. Behold, I make all things ___. (Rev. 21:5)
63. Kimono sashes.
64. ___ he break out like fire in the house. (Amos 5:6)
65. Let us search and ___ our ways. (Lam. 3:40)

Down

1. He ___ the blameless in His way. (2 Sam. 22:33, ASV)
2. As it were ___ [2 words] of glass. (Rev. 15:2)
3. Lord, let it alone this ___ also. (Luke 13:8)
4. The angel of the LORD protested unto ___. (Zech. 3:6)
5. I am like an ___ of the desert. (Ps. 102:6)
6. Since the days of ___-haddon king of Assur. (Ezra 4:2)
7. Ussiah the king was a ___. (2 Chron. 26:21)
8. A fool's work ___ him. (Eccles. 10:15, NIV)
9. Do ye not therefore ___, because you know not the scriptures. (Mark 12:24)
10. ___ the kine to the cart. (1 Sam. 6:7)
11. He rebuketh the ___, and maketh it dry. (Nah. 1:4)
19. Be in health, even ___ thy soul prospereth. (3 John 2)
21. Indian mulberry.
23. In the ___ of the sabbath, as it began to dawn toward the first day. (Matt. 28:1)
25. The LORD will smite with a ___ the crown. (Isa. 3:17)

26. Roof edge.
27. Their blood have they ___ like water. (Ps. 79:3)
28. Scottish names prefix.
29. Anab, and Eshtemoh, and ___. (Josh. 15:50)
30. ___ hath no part nor inheritance. (Deut. 10:9)
32. "___ the season to be jolly."
35. The Holy Ghost also is a ___ to us. (Heb. 10:15)
37. We ___ our bread with the peril of our lives. (Lam. 5:9)
40. Pasture.
42. Jesus ___ is come in the flesh. (1 John 4:2)

45. And after the fire a ___ small voice. (1 Kings 19:12)
47. Dawn (comb. form).
49. Healing herb.
51. My people are ___ to backsliding. (Hos. 11:7)
52. Eat, and live for ___. (Gen. 3:22)
53. Moist.
54. Wisdom is ___ high for a fool. (Prov. 24:7)
55. The spear smote him under the fifth ___. (2 Sam. 2:23)
56. Samuel feared to show ___ the vision. (1 Sam. 3:15)
58. Jesse took an ___ laden with bread. (1 Sam. 16:20)

22

Across

1. Provide yourselves ___ which wax not old. (Luke 12:33)
5. Carried the sick on ____ to wherever they heard he was. (Mark 6:55, NIV)
9. I ___ three unclean spirits like frogs. (Rev. 16:13)
12. Small fish.
13. Air (comb. form).
14. Woman's name.
15. ___ of Cana in Galilee. (John 21:2)
17. They ___ my path, they set forward my calamity. (Job 30:13)
18. Not as Cain, who was of that wicked ___. (1 John 3:12)
19. Scents.
21. God shall ___ at thee with an arrow. (Ps. 64:7)
24. Can a ___ open the eyes of the blind? (John 10:21, NIV)
26. Ye rich men, weep and ___ for your miseries. (James 5:1)
27. A mighty man of ___, a warrior, one prudent in speech, and a handsome man. (1 Sam. 16:18, ASV)
28. Egyptian sun god.
30. Praise our God, ___ ye his servants. (Rev. 19:5)
31. Your braided hair shines like the finest ___. (Song 7:5, GNB)
32. Elijah went up to the ___ of Carmel. (1 Kings 18:42)
33. Shew ___ thy faith without thy works. (James 2:18)
34. Number all the firstborn of the ___. (Num. 3:40)
35. Look to other ___, and love flagons of wine. (Hos. 3:1)
36. Their words seemed to them as idle ___. (Luke 24:11)
37. Many bodies of the saints which slept ___. (Matt. 27:52)
38. Be self-controlled and ___. (1 Peter 5:8, NIV)
40. Tossed to and ___, and carried about with every wind of doctrine. (Eph. 4:14)
41. The younger, she also bare a son, and called his name ___-Ammi. (Gen. 19:38)
42. A man of knowledge ___ strength. (Prov. 24:5, NIV)
48. I'll ___ each one of you a piece of fine linen. (Judg. 14:12, GNB)
49. Neither . . . flattering words, as ye know, ___ [2 words] cloke of covetousness. (1 Thess. 2:5)
50. ___ the eighth person, a preacher. (2 Peter 2:5)
51. He planteth an ___, and the rain doth nourish it. (Isa. 44:4)
52. Cymric deity.
53. Make your calling and election ___. (2 Peter 1:10)

Down

1. I will consign Jacob to the ___. (Isa. 43:28, ASV)
2. In the manner of (French).
3. ___ thee quickly out of Jerusalem. (Acts 22:18)
4. Disputing daily in the ___ of one Tyrannus. (Acts 19:9)
5. Clothe his neck with a flowing ___. (Job 39:19, NIV)
6. Jephunneh, and Pispah, and ___. (1 Chron. 7:38)
7. Wooden stand.
8. But ___ built him an house. (Acts 7:47)
9. Blessed art thou, ___ Bar-jona. (Matt. 16:17)
10. The twelfth month, that is, the month ___. (Esther 3:7)
11. Ye shall hear of ___ and commotions. (Luke 21:9)
16. Go to the ___, thou sluggard. (Prov. 6:6)
20. The son of Abinadab, in all the region of ___. (1 Kings 4:11)
21. Counterfeit.
22. Hide it there in a ___ of the rock. (Jer. 13:4)

1
2
3
4
5
6
7
8
9
10
11
12
13
14
15
16
17
18
19
20
21
22
23
24
25
26
27
28
29
30
31
32
33
34
35
36
37
38
39
40
41
42
43
44
45
46
47
48
49
50
51
52
53

23. The screech ___ also shall rest there. (Isa. 34:14)
24. It is not for you to know the times or ___. (Acts 1:7, NIV)
25. The iniquity of ___ house shall not be purged. (1 Sam. 3:14)
27. The ___ of Siddim was full of slimepits. (Gen. 14:10)
28. Aaron's rod swallowed up their ___. (Exod. 7:12)
29. Bishop's seat.
31. Seasoning.
32. But the priests were ___ few. (2 Chron. 29:34)
34. After this manner will I ___ the pride of Judah. (Jer. 13:9)
35. With ___ that words cannot express. (Rom. 8:26, NIV)
36. I will surely give the ___ unto thee. (Gen. 28:22)
37. They ___ gone into captivity from thee. (Mic. 1:6)
38. ___, Father, all things are possible unto thee; take away this cup from me. (Mark 14:36)
39. He hath settled on his ___, and hath not been emptied. (Jer. 48:11)
40. Girl's name.
43. This is ___ bone of my bones. (Gen. 2:23)
44. Whereby we ___, Abba, Father. (Rom. 8:15)
45. Old French coin.
46. LORD, bow down thine ___, and hear. (2 Kings 19:16)
47. ___ was found with child of the Holy Ghost. (Matt. 1:18)

23

Across

1. ___ the labourers, and give them their hire. (Matt. 20:8)
5. We have ___ all, and have followed thee. (Mark 10:28)
9. ___ sent Joram his son unto king David. (2 Sam. 8:10)
12. Athena's title.
13. Heraldic wreath.
14. Head covering.
15. And the sons of Calib: Iru, Elah, and ___. (1 Chron. 4:15)
16. I know not: Am I my ___ keeper? (Gen. 4:9)
18. A man that is clean shall gather up the ___ of the heifer. (Num. 19:9)
20. P. K. ___ (Indian poet).
21. At thy word I will let down the ___. (Luke 5:5)
23. The ___ of God was upon the cities. (Gen. 35:5)
27. No man can serve two ___. (Matt. 6:24)
31. Give account to him that is ___ to judge the quick and the dead. (1 Peter 4:5)
32. And the sons of Gad; Ziphion and Haggi, Shuni, and Ezbon, ___, and Arodi. (Gen. 46:16)
33. ___ once more I shake not the earth only. (Heb. 12:26)
35. Black-tailed gazelle.
36. Is it ___ for you to flog a Roman? (Acts 22:25, NIV)
39. Holder of light.
42. He lodgeth with one Simon a ___. (Acts 10:6)
44. They have no rest day ___ night. (Rev. 14:11)
45. Kildare's capital.
47. The creation ___ in eager expectation for the sons of God to be revealed. (Rom. 8:19, NIV)
51. Others ___, "He seems to be advocating foreign gods." (Acts 17:18, NIV)

Down

55. Mine ___ hath done them, and my graven image. (Isa. 48:5)
56. For by grace ___ ye saved through faith. (Eph. 2:8)
57. Let us draw ___ with a true heart. (Heb. 10:22)
58. Paul was brought before ___. (2 Tim. subscript)
59. No ___ hath seen God at any time. (1 John 4:12)
60. Fast transports.
61. They ___ together by course in praising. (Ezra 3:11)

Down

1. There was a marriage in ___ of Galilee. (John 2:1)
2. ___ for the day! for the day of the LORD is at hand. (Joel 1:15)
3. ___ was tender eyed. (Gen. 29:17)
4. Ye shall weep and ___, but the world shall rejoice. (John 16:20)
5. Highly arced toss.
6. He who makes haste with his feet ___. (Prov. 19:2, ASV)
7. Elisha cut a stick and threw it there, and made the iron ___. (2 Kings 6:6, NIV)
8. He will ___ his donkey to a vine. (Gen. 49:11, NIV)
9. Cometh to ___ thousand three hundred and five and thirty days. (Dan. 12:12)
10. All that handle the ___, the mariners. (Ezek. 27:29)
11. That which groweth of ___ own accord. (Lev. 25:5)
17. The ___, because he cheweth the cud. (Lev. 11:6)
19. I ___ the heavens opened, and the Son of man standing on the right hand of God. (Acts 7:56)
22. To ___ them that dwell upon the earth. (Rev. 3:10)
24. The chariots shall ___ in the streets. (Nah. 2:4)

25. By this time there is a bad ___.
    (John 11:39, NIV)
26. Man's name.
27. The elements shall ___ with fervent
    heat. (2 Peter 3:10)
28. He has brought Greeks into the
    temple ___. (Acts 21:28, NIV)
29. Wherefore tongues are for a ___. (1
    Cor. 14:22)
30. Salt (French).
34. Light brown.
37. There was one ___, a prophetess
    (Luke 2:36)
38. When he ___ of it he will be guilty.
    (Lev. 5:3, NIV)
40. Beloved, ___ are we the sons of
    God. (1 John 3:2)

41. The LORD, my Rock, who ___ my
    hands for war. (Ps. 144:1, NIV)
43. Gathering instruments.
46. The Pharisees sit in Moses' ___.
    (Matt. 23:2)
48. The Lord has sent me to do all these
    things and that it was not my ___.
    (Num. 16:28, NIV)
49. Ye brought that which was ___, and
    the lame. (Mal. 1:3)
50. To walk slowly.
51. Elihu the son of Barachel the Buzite,
    of the kindred of ___. (Job 32:2)
52. Time period.
53. ___ blasphemed God because of
    the plague. (Rev. 16:21)
54. Medical appelations (abbr.).

24

Across

1. With the ___ of an ass have I slain a thousand men. (Judg. 15:16)
4. Thy ___ and thy she goats have not cast their young. (Gen. 31:38)
8. He saith also in ___, I will call them my people. (Rom. 9:25)
12. Carbohydrate.
13. This do ye; ___ your beasts, and go. (Gen. 45:17)
14. Neither ___ you up a standing image. (Lev. 26:1)
15. Ye shall speak into the ___. (1 Cor. 14:9)
16. Thou art a swift ___ traversing her ways. (Jer. 2:23)
18. He shall wash his clothes, and ___ himself. (Lev. 15:8)
20. Intrigue (Italian).
21. He planteth an ___, and the rain doth nourish it. (Isa. 44:14)
23. Imbeciles.
27. Legume.
30. The valley of Giddim was full of ___ pits. (Gen. 14:10, NIV)
32. As a ___ which melteth. (Ps. 58:8)
33. ___ my tears on your scroll. (Ps. 56:8, NIV)
35. ___, thy sins be forgiven thee. (Mark 2:5)
37. Snow runner (phonetic).
38. He assigned ___ unto a place where he knew that valiant men were. (2 Sam. 11:16)
40. One of the dwarfs.
42. Direction: Jerusalem to Bethlehem [5 miles].
43. Bringer of food.
45. I answered, ___ art thou, Lord? (Acts 22:8)
47. They came to ___, where were twelve wells. (Exod. 15:27)
49. They that feared the Lord spake ___ one to another. (Mal. 3:16)
53. Jesus sat at meat in the ___ house. (Luke 7:37)
57. I ___ no pleasant bread. (Dan. 10:3)
58. Upon the wicked he shall ___ snares. (Ps. 11:6)
59. Etham, in the ___ of the wilderness. (Exod. 13:20)
60. After this manner will I ___ the pride of Judah. (Jer. 13:9)
61. The hired hand is not the shepherd who ___ the sheep. (John 10:12, NIV)
62. The woman ought to have a ___ of authority on her head. (1 Cor. 11:10, NIV)
63. The sons of ___, Hophni and Phinehas. (1 Sam. 1:3)

Down

1. Abishai the son of Zeruish, brother to ___. (1 Sam. 26:6)
2. The churches of ___ salute you. (1 Cor. 16:19)
3. If thou ___ cut out of the olive tree which is wild by nature. (Rom. 11:24)
4. Reuben, the ___ son of Israel. (Num. 26:5)
5. He doth judge and make ___. (Rev. 19:11)
6. ___ saith, We are impoverished. (Mal. 1:4)
7. Mattathias, which was the son of ___. (Luke 3:26)
8. Confers holy orders.
9. The horse and his rider hath he thrown into the ___. (Exod. 15:21)
10. He touched his ___, and healed him. (Luke 22:51)
11. State of (suffix).
17. Be for salvation unto the ___ of the earth. (Acts 13:47)
19. ___; and he smelleth the battle afar off. (Job 39:25)
22. To render to every man according to what he ___ done. (Rev. 22:12, ASV)
24. He was strong as the ___. (Amos 2:9)
25. I led them with cords of human kindness, with ___ of love. (Hos. 11:4, NIV)

26. He ___ two lionlike men of Moab. (2 Sam. 23:20)
27. He shall make restitution for his trespass in full value ___ one-fifth of it. (Num. 5:7, NKJ)
28. Ireland.
29. Saudi Arabian district.
31. The ___ and reproof give wisdom. (Prov. 29:15)
34. They came to meet us as far as Appii forum, and The Three ___. (Acts 28:15)
36. ___ is come salvation, and strength. (Rev. 12:10)
39. The son of Joseph, which was the son of ___. (Luke 3:23)
41. Hath not God ___ the poor of this world? (James 2:5)

44. The morning star ___ in your hearts. (2 Peter 1:19, NIV)
46. Simon's wife's mother lay sick ___ a fever. (Mark 1:30)
48. Middle (comb. form).
50. Neither could any man ___ him. (Mark 5:4)
51. And others (Latin).
52. Salathaiel, which was the son of ___. (Luke 3:27)
53. Opposite amateur.
54. Left command.
55. Riblah, on the east side of ___. (Num. 34:11)
56. Is there any taste in the white of an ___? (Job 6:6)

25

Across

1. If her father had but ___ in her face. (Num. 12:14)
5. The Spirit of life from ___ entered into them. (Rev. 11:11)
8. Thou has bought me no sweet ___ with money. (Isa. 43:24)
12. Master, the Jews of ___ sought to stone thee. (John 11:8)
13. Genetic structure.
14. Of ___, the family of Arodites. ((Num. 26:17)
15. An irreducible constituent.
16. Indefinitely long time period.
17. I will put my laws ___ in their mind. (Heb. 8:10)
18. The Lord shall judge his ___ . (Heb. 10:30)
20. Lower in temperature.
22. ___ your moderation be known unto all. (Phil. 4:5)
23. The poor man had nothing, save one little ___ lamb. (2 Sam. 12:3)
24. If you hit someone's nose, it ___. (Prov. 30:33, GNB)
27. To ___ them that were under the law. (Gal. 4:5)
31. Their villages were Etam, and ___, and Rimmon, and Tochan, and Ashan. (1 Chron. 4:32)
32. The sons of Jether, Jephunnah, and Pispah, and ___. (1 Chron. 7:38)
33. About midnight the shipmen ___ that they drew near to some country. (Acts 27:27)
37. Why eateth your ___ with publicans and sinners? (Matt. 9:11)
40. More bitter than beer.
41. Historical time period.
42. Speaking to yourselves in ___ and hymns. (Eph. 5:19)
45. Their soul is ___ because of trouble. (Ps. 107:26)
49. Places (Lat.).
50. Their lives ___ away in their mothers' arms. (Lam. 2:12, NIV)

52. They told you there should be mockers in the last ___.(Jude 18)
53. Long, narrative poem.
54. It shall be as the chased ___. (Isa. 13:14)
55. The sons of Ram the firstborn of Jerahmeel were, Maaz, and Jamin, and ___. (1 Chron. 2:27)
56. Hartebeest.
57. They used brick instead of stone, and ___ for mortar. (Gen. 11:3, NIV)
58. Levee.

Down

1. They crowd around me and ___ my face. (Job 16:10, GNB)
2. His violent dealing shall come down upon his own ___. (Ps. 7:16)
3. Through her ___ [2 words] may have children. (Gen. 30:3, ASV)
4. No man was able to enter into the ___. (Rev. 15:8)
5. If anyone ___ you, do not answer. (2 Kings 4:29, NIV)
6. The children of Lod, Hadid, and ___. (Ezra 2:33)
7. Herodias' daughter's occupation. (Mark 6:22)
8. Jesus, which is ___ Justus. (Col. 4:11)
9. It goes through ___ places seeking rest. (Matt. 12:43, NIV)
10. Give ___ occasion to the adversary. (1 Tim. 5:14)
11. Southward were Kabzeel, and ___, and Jagur. (Josh. 15:21)
19. If ye be ___ of the Spirit, ye are not under the law. (Gal. 5:18)
21. ___ no man anything. (Rom. 13:8)
24. Jerusalem, building the rebellious and the ___ city. (Ezra 4:12)
25. Hath Satan filled thine heart to ___. (Acts 5:3)
26. Direction: Emmaus to Jericho [19 miles].

28. Rise, Peter; kill and ___. (Acts 10:13)

29. How long will it be ___ they believe me? (Num. 14:11)

30. They ___ my path, they set forward my calamity, they have no helper. (Job 30:13)

34. In ___ be ye children but in understanding be men. (1 Cor. 14:20)

35. O.T. tree (mentioned in Hosea 4:13).

36. He led the flock to the backside of the ___. (Exod. 3:1)

37. For the body is not one ___. (1 Cor. 12:14)

38. They blaspheme that worthy name by which ye ___ called. (James 2:7)

39. For every one shall be ___ with fire. (Mark 9:49)

42. Hear their prayer and their ___. (1 Kings 8:49, NIV)

43. Soaks up.

44. Galatea's beloved.

46. Polynesian idol.

47. The valley of Jiphthah-al toward the north side of Beth- ___, and Neiel. (Josh. 19:27)

48. Harm (Old English).

51. Feathery scarf.

26

Across

1. The lion had not eaten the carcase, nor torn the ___. (1 Kings 13:28)
4. Nevertheless ___ heart was perfect. (1 Kings 15:14)
8. I have ___ sackcloth over my skin. (Job 16:15, NKJ)
12. That he hath no oblation chooseth a tree that will not ___. (Isa. 40:20)
13. Call me not Naomi, call me ___. (Ruth 1:20)
14. Algonquin Indian.
15. Reserved in heaven for you, who ___ kept by the power of God through faith. (1 Peter 1:4–5)
16. Ships . . . shall afflict ___, and he also shall perish for ever. (Num. 24:24)
17. The veil of the temple was ___ in twain. (Mark 15:38)
18. ___ that thou forget not the Lord. (Deut. 8:11)
20. Pochereth of Zebaim, the children of ___. (Ezra 2:57)
22. Organization under the F.C.A.
23. In the ___ tongue Armageddon. (Rev. 16:16)
27. Whoever ___ to me will live in safety. (Prov. 1:33, NIV)
31. Shall any ___ God knowledge? (Job 21:22)
32. ___ the son of Ikkesh the Tekoite. (2 Sam. 23:26)
33. The trees of the LORD are full of ___. (Ps. 104:16)
35. There should be mockers in ___ last time. (Jude 18)
36. Covers with harder material.
39. Athaliah rent her clothes, and cried, ___. (2 Kings 11:14)
42. He ___ the battle from afar. (Job 39:25, NKJ)
44. The ___ of all things is at hand. (1 Peter 4:7)
45. Every ___ shall see him. (Rev. 1:7)
46. To ___, if it were possible, even the elect. (Mark 13:22)
50. Pole.
53. School type (abbr.).

Down

55. ___ hands suddenly on no man. (1 Tim. 5:22)
56. What I ___, that do I. (Rom. 7:15)
57. My brethren, be not ___ masters. (James 3:1)
58. They divine a ___ unto thee. (Ezek. 21:29)
59. The land of Nod, on the east of ___. (Gen. 4:16)
60. Thanks to him who ___ on the throne. (Rev. 4:9, NIV)
61. Town near Liege.

Down

1. ___, and Dumah, and Eshean. (Josh. 15:52)
2. For he is lunatick, and ___ vexed. (Matt. 17:15)
3. Jacob gave Esau some bread and some lentil ___. (Gen. 25:34, NIV)
4. They shall ___ him in an hundred shekels. (Deut. 22:19)
5. They shall sell them [children] to the ___. (Joel 3:8)
6. They ___ no more twain, but one flesh. (Mark 10:8)
7. Lo, ___ thy wife shall have a son. (Gen. 18:10)
8. Where is the wise? where is the ___? (1 Cor. 1:20)
9. How long will it be ___ thou be quiet? (Jer. 47:6)
10. Maimed, or having a ___, or scurvy. (Lev. 22:22)
11. The wicked desireth the ___ of evil men. (Prov. 12:12)
19. All that were strong and ___ for war. (2 Kings 24:16)
21. Mercy and truth are ___ together. (Ps. 85:10)
24. Make models of the tumors and of the ___ that are destroying the country. (1 Sam. 6:5, NIV)
25. The beams of the woodwork will ___ it. (Hab. 2:11, NIV)
26. ___ I was a child, I spake as a child. (1 Cor. 13:11)

27. Righteous ___ are the delight of kings. (Prov. 16:13)

28. Duke Magdiel, duke ___: these be the dukes of Edom. (Gen. 36:43)

29. The Son of man is come to ___ that which was lost. ((Matt. 18:11)

30. Now Peter ___ without in the palace. (Matt. 26:69)

34. That I may ___ you as a chaste virgin. (2 Cor. 11:2)

37. Then the ___ disciples went away. (Matt. 28:16)

38. They plotted to arrest Jesus in some ___ way and kill him. (Matt. 26:4, NIV)

40. Deliver me from the ___ hand. (Job 6:23)

41. Ye intend to ___ more to our sins. (2 Chron. 28:13)

43. He ___ to be advocating foreign gods. (Acts 17:18, NIV)

47. The sons of ___; Arah, and Haniel. (1 Chron. 7:39)

48. ___ was a tiller of the ground. (Gen. 4:2)

49. His ___ were as a flame of fire. (Rev. 19:12)

50. And ___ brought forth a man child. (Rev. 12:5)

51. Let it not be grievous in thy sight because of the ___. (Gen. 21:12)

52. They joined themselves . . . , and ___ the sacrifices of the dead. (Ps. 106:28)

54. Medieval tale.

27

Across

1. The imagination of ___ heart is evil. (Gen. 8:21)
5. I ___ daily with you teaching in the temple. (Matt. 26:55)
8. Miami's county.
12. And after him was Shammah the son of ___. (2 Sam. 23:11)
13. Jephunneh, and Pispah, and ___. (1 Chron. 7:38)
14. Elijah went to shew himself unto ___. (1 Kings 18:2)
15. Hur, and ___, five kings of Midian. (Num. 31:8)
16. Thou shalt in any wise let the ___ go. (Deut. 22:7)
17. Halo.
18. The angel of the Lord ___ him, because he gave not God the glory. (Acts 12:23)
20. The leaves of the tree were for the healing of the ___. (Rev. 22:2)
22. Tree mentioned in Hosea 4:13.
24. Let her be as the loving hind and pleasant ___. (Prov. 5:19)
25. Athletic arena.
29. My arm be broken off at the ___. (Job 31:22, ASV)
33. I saw Absalom hanged in an ___. (2 Sam. 18:10)
34. ___ shall be a serpent by the way. (Gen. 49:17)
36. The poor man had nothing, save one little ___ lamb. (2 Sam. 12:3)
37. In the ___ they gathered salt herbs. (Job 30:4, NIV)
40. Your navel is a ___ goblet. (Song of Sol. 7:2, NIV)
43. They have digged a ___ for my soul. (Jer. 18:20)
45. Direction: Emmaus (Nicopolis) to Jerusalem [15 mi].
46. The book of creation.
50. The creation waits in ___ expectation. (Rom. 8:19, NIV)
54. Am I ___, [2 words] or a whale? (Job 7:12)

55. For since by ___ came death. (1 Cor. 15:21)
57. We will ___ upon the swift. (Isa. 30:16)
58. Have ye not fulfilled your ___ in making brick both yesterday and to day? (Exod. 5:14)
59. Direction: Jerusalem to Jericho [15 miles].
60. Walk, ___ as he walked. (1 John 2:6)
61. Your land by the sea will become open fields with shepherd's ___ and sheep pens.(Zeph. 2:6, GNB)
62. I do ___ my bow in the cloud. (Gen. 9:13)
63. Caused depression.

Down

1. Paul stood in the midst of ___ hill. (Acts 17:22)
2. The way ___ [2 words] cutter engraves a seal. (Exod. 28:11, NIV)
3. Bel boweth down, ___ stoopeth. (Isa. 46:1)
4. In a portion of the lawgiver, was he ___. (Deut. 33:21)
5. As ye walk and are ___. (Luke 24:17)
6. The sons of Dishan; Uz and ___. (1 Chron. 1:42)
7. I love ___, my brother Absalom's sister. (2 Sam. 6:4)
8. But thou, O ___, shut up the words. (Dan. 12:4)
9. The ark of God: ___ went before the ark. (2 Sam. 6:4)
10. To doom as judgment.
11. Now my life ___ away. (Job 30:16, NIV)
19. The ark of God was taken; and the two sons of ___. (1 Sam. 4:11)
21. Upon the great ___ of their right foot. (Exod. 28:20)
23. Jeremiah sank down into the ___. (Jer. 38:6, NIV)
25. My soul will ___ in secret. (Job 13:17, ASV)

26. They used brick instead of stone, and ___ for mortar. (Gen. 11:3, NIV)
27. Hawaiian fish.
28. They ___ my path, they set forward my calamity. (Job 30:13)
30. He deviseth mischief upon his ___. (Ps. 36:4)
31. ___ no man any thing. (Rom. 13:8)
32. I will judge thee, as women that break ___ lock. (Ezek. 16:38)
35. Until that day the ___ entered into the ark. (Matt. 24:38)
38. He who ___ from himself seeks his own glory. (John 7:18, NKJ)
39. Every man according to ___ several ability. (Matt. 25:15)
41. In vain shalt thou ___ many medicines. (Jer. 46:11)
42. Approached.

44. A friend loveth at all ___. (Prov. 17:17)
46. The Philistine of ___, Goliath by name. (1 Sam. 17:23)
47. Lest there by any fornicator, or profane person, as ___. (Heb. 12:16)
48. Then I said, I shall die in my ___. (Job 29:18)
49. Or are we ___? It is for your sake. (2 Cor. 5:13, GNB)
51. I will ___ you pastors according to mine heart. (Jer. 3:15)
52. God planted a garden eastward in ___. (Gen. 2:8)
53. The veil of the temple was ___ in twain. (Matt. 27:51)
56. The fishes that are taken in an evil ___. (Eccles. 9:12)

28

Across

1. Jonathan was very ___ of David. (1 Sam. 19:1, NIV)
5. He hath ___ his bow like an enemy. (Lam. 2:4)
9. There was war between ___ and Baasha. (1 Kings 15:32)
12. His foul ___ will rise, because he has done monstrous things. (Joel 2:20, NKJ)
13. Deliver thyself as ___ [2 words] from the hunter. (Prov. 6:5)
14. The eyes of Israel were ___ for age. (Gen. 48:10)
15. No one ___ you when he is dead. (Ps. 6:5, NIV)
17. Why make ye this ___, and weep? (Mark 5:39)
18. The righteous also shall ___, and fear. (Ps. 52:6)
19. God, who at sundry ___ and in divers manners spake in time past. (Heb. 1:1)
21. Who am less than the ___ of all saints. (Eph. 3:8)
24. There was ___ in his temple the ark. (Rev. 11:19)
26. His soul shall dwell at ___. (Ps. 25:13)
27. Such as wrought iron and brass to ___ the house of the Lord. (2 Chron. 24:12)
28. God will hear all the words of ___ - shakeh (2 Kings 19:4).
31. Anna, a prophetess, the daughter of Phanuel, of the tribe of ___. (Luke 2:36)
32. Despise dominion, ___ speak evil of dignities. (Jude 8)
33. Distant prefix.
34. Education group.
35. Very (French).
36. ___ it, even to the foundation thereof. (Ps. 137:7)
37. Adam . . . begat a son in his own likeness, after his image; and called his name ___. (Gen. 5:3)
38. Is not ___ the Levite thy brother? (Exod. 4:14)

39. His fame went throughout all ___. (Matt. 4:24)
42. Haggi, Shuni, and Ezbon, ___, and Arodi. (Gen. 46:16)
43. We sailed to the ___ of Crete. (Acts 27:7, NIV)
44. Simon the ___, and Judas Iscariot. (Matt. 10:4)
50. God shall wipe away ___ tears. (Rev. 21:4)
51. So the tabernacle was a ___. (Exod. 36:13, ASV)
52. Financial course (abbr.).
53. Will ___ her trade with all the kingdoms on the face of the earth. (Isa. 23:17, NIV)
54. Books of ecclesiastical rules.
55. But will God in very ___ dwell with men on the earth? (2 Chron. 6:18)

Down

1. Abraham believed God, and it was imputed unto him ___ righteousness. (James 2:23)
2. Lyric poem of praise.
3. Name (French).
4. Then said he unto the ___ of his vineyard. (Luke 13:7)
5. She saw the child: and, behold, the ___ wept. (Exod. 2:6)
6. How long will it be ___ they believe me? (Num. 14:11)
7. Whom no man hath seen, ___ can see. (1 Tim. 6:16)
8. Some time later God ___ Abraham. (Gen. 22:1, NIV)
9. I covered my transgressions as ___. (Job 31:33)
10. The wicked walk on every ___. (Ps. 12:8)
11. Amaziah said unto ___, O thou seer. (Amos 7:12)
16. Mercy and truth are ___ together. (Ps. 85:10)
20. Whosoever believeth ___ him should not perish. (John 3:15)
21. Why ___ ye, ye high hills? (Ps. 68:16)

1	2	3	4		5	6	7	8		9	10	11
12					13					14		
15			16							17		
		18					19	20				
21	22	23			24	25						
26				27				28	29	30
31				32			33			
34			35				36			
		37				38				
39	40	41			42					
43			44	45	46			47	48	49
50			51					52		
53			54					55		

22. The lightning cometh out of the ___. (Matt. 24:27)

23. There was ___[2 words] of glass like unto crystal. (Rev. 4:6)

24. The name of the one was Bozez, and the name of the other ___. (1 Sam. 14:4)

25. The Creator of the ___ of the earth. (Isa. 40:28)

27. She is a ___ of nations. (Isa. 23:3)

28. Wilt thou ___ it up in three days? (John 2:20)

29. He made the stars ___. (Gen. 1:16)

30. The LORD hath ___ mindful of us. (Ps. 115:12)

33. He armed his ___ servants. (Gen. 14:14)

35. Fine beverage container.

37 Yes (Spanish).

38. Jephunneh, and Pispah, and ___. (1 Chron. 7:38)

39. Let him ___ your left cheek too. (Matt. 5:39, GNB)

40. They shall ___ as lions' whelps. (Jer. 51:38)

41. Because thou didst ___ on the LORD. (2 Chron. 16:8)

42. All his days he ___ in darkness. (Eccles. 5:17, NIV)

45. See thou nothing to ___ man. (Mark 1:44)

46. Never (German).

47. He casteth forth his ___ like morsels. (Ps. 147:17)

48. Upon the great ___ of his right foot. (Lev. 14:14)

49. For Christ is the ___ of the law. (Rom. 10:4)

29

Across

1. The coat was without ___. (John 19:23)
5. Direction: Joppa to Jerusalem [33 miles].
8. Then the children shall tremble from the ___. (Hos. 11:10)
12. Tanning tree.
13. Why does he eat with ___ collectors? (Mark 2:16)
14. Oil (comb. form).
15. The first beast was like a ___. (Rev. 4:7)
16. Go to the ___, thou sluggard. (Prov. 6:6)
17. The ___ which is lent to the LORD. (1 Sam. 2:20)
18. General tendency.
20. His children in subjection with all ___. (1 Tim. 3:4)
22. He touched his ___, and healed him. (Luke 22:51)
24. Do those things which ___ not convenient. (Rom. 1:28)
25. The ___ God is thy refuge. (Deut. 33:27)
29. Out of ___, his bread shall be fat. (Gen. 49:20)
33. ___ is come salvation, and strength, and the kingdom of our God. (Rev. 12:10)
34. Tuesday's namesake.
36. ___ the son of Ikkesh the Tekoite. (2 Sam. 23:26)
37. Thou hatest the ___ of the Nicolaitanes. (Rev. 2:6)
40. Shewing thyself a ___ of good works. (Tit. 2:7)
43. There was no power in the ___. (Dan. 8:7)
45. ___, give me this water, that I thirst not. (John 4:15)
46. Not given to wine, no ___, not greedy. (1 Tim. 3:3)
50. The ___ opened her mouth, and swallowed up the flood. (Rev. 12:16)
54. Indian tribe.

55. Wilt dash their children, and ___ up their women with child. (2 Kings 8:12)
57. He set it up in the plain of ___. (Dan. 3:1)
58. With one look of your eye, with one ___ of your necklace. (Song of Sol. 4:9, NKJ)
59. Unto Baal-peor, and ___ the sacrifices of the dead. (Ps. 106:28)
60. All the trees of ___, the choice and best. (Ezek. 31:16)
61. They hatch cockatrice' ___, and weave the spider's web. (Isa. 59:5)
62. She called his name ___ -oni; but his father called him Benjamin. (Gen. 35:18)
63. This man shall be blessed in his ___. (James 1:25)

Down

1. Have ___ in yourselves. (Mark 9:50)
2. Arabian prince.
3. Healing plant.
4. I speak after the ___ of men. (Gal. 3:15)
5. Terminal abbreviation.
6. Is not this David, of whom they ___? (1 Sam. 29:5)
7. Wear sandals but not an ___ tunic. (Mark 6:9, NIV)
8. Behold, I send you forth as lambs among the ___. (Luke 10:3)
9. ___, lama sabacthani? (Mark 15:34)
10. Said Paul, I stand at Caesar's judgment ___. (Acts 25:10)
11. Nickname for Anthony.
19. ___ shall judge his people. (Gen. 49:16)
21. Jephunneh, and Pispah, and ___. (1 Chron. 7:38)
23. Unclean for you: the weasel, the ___. (Lev. 11:29, NIV)
25. The harvest is the ___ of the world. (Matt. 13:39)
26. And on the big ___ of his right foot. (Lev. 14:28, NIV)

27. What mean these seven ___ lambs? (Gen. 21:29)

28. They shoot out the ___, they shake the head. (Ps. 22:7)

30. Haste.

31. They ___ in vision, they stumble in judgment. (Isa. 28:7)

32. The water ___ round about the altar. (2 Kings 18:35, RSV)

35. Jesus Christ our Lord, which ___ made of the seed of David. (Rom. 1:3)

38. Which stood only in meats and ___, and divers washings. (Heb. 9:10)

39. Egyptian cotton.

41. ___ them in bundles to be burned. (Matt. 13:30, NIV)

42. With silver, iron, tin, and lead, they ___ in thy fairs. (Ezek. 27:12)

44. ___ Saul's daughter should have been given to David. (1 Sam. 18:19)

46. Let him count the years of the ___ thereof. (Lev. 25:27)

47. Like a ___ on the surface of the waters. (Hos. 10:7, NIV)

48. Israel shouted with a great shout, so that the earth ___ again. (1 Sam. 4:5)

49. He must do so according to the ___ of Passover. (Num. 9:14, NKJ)

51. Though I be ___ of speech. (2 Cor. 11:6)

52. Every ___ is known by his own fruit. (Luke 6:44)

53. For the time is at ___. (Rev. 22:10)

56. Out of Zebulun they that handle the ___ of the writer. (Judg. 5:14)

30

Across

1. ___ told Jezebel all that Elijah had done. (1 Kings 19:1)
5. Educational organization.
8. They shall surely ask counsel at ___. (2 Sam. 20:18)
12. The foundation of God standeth ___. (2 Tim. 2:19)
13. Is any among you afflicted? let ___ pray. (James 5:13)
14. Send ye the lamb to the ruler of the land from ___. (Isa. 16:1)
15. Be like a gazelle or like a young ___. (Song of Sol. 2:17, NIV)
16. And ___, five; heads of the house of their fathers. (1 Chron. 7:7)
17. Barzillai was a very ___ man. (2 Sam. 19:32)
18. ___ ye have believed in vain. (1 Cor. 15:2)
21. He casteth forth his ___ like morsels. (Ps. 147:17)
22. LXX's 'Kurios,' meaning 'LORD.'
25. There was ___ in his temple the ark. (Rev. 11:19)
27. Beloved, ___ are we the sons of God. (1 John 3:2)
28. Second postscript.
30. ___ and Caiaphas being the high priests. (Luke 3:2)
33. There was one ___, a prophetess. (Luke 2:36)
35. ___, didst not thou sow good seed? (Matt. 13:27)
37. Billion (comb. form).
38. Refuge for the slayer; and ___ - terah. (Josh. 21:27)
40. Behold, I make all things ___. (Rev. 21:5)
42. His servant Joshua, the son of ___. (Exod. 33:11)
43. That this epistle be ___ unto all the holy brethren. (1 Thess. 5:27)
45. The likeness of any ___ fowl that flieth. (Deut. 4:17)
47. Wine cup.

49. Called the council together, and all the ___ of the children of Israel. (Acts 5:21)
51. He ___ his birthright unto Jacob. (Gen. 25:33)
53. Persian native.
54. The ___ of the temple was rent in twain. (Mark 15:38)
58. Take thine ___, eat, drink, and be merry. (Luke 12:19)
59. But not of my spirit, that they may ___ sin to sin. (Isa. 30:1)
60. Sea falcon.
61. The word, and ___ with joy receiveth it. (Matt. 13:20)
62. Doth your master pay tribute? He saith, ___. (Matt. 17:24–25)
63. ___ your heart, and not your garments. (Joel 2:13)

Down

1. Doth the wild ___ bray? (Job 6:5)
2. It sways like a ___ in the wind. (Isa. 24:20, NIV)
3. The son of Jether; Jephunneh, and Pispah, and ___. (1 Chron. 7:38)
4. The plague was ___ among the people. (Num. 16:47)
5. Being reproved by him for Herodias his brother ___ wife. (Luke 3:19)
6. Never ___ of doing what is right. (2 Thess. 3:13, NIV)
7. We have sinned, we have done ___. (2 Chron. 6:37)
8. ___ cut down her idol, and stamped it. (2 Chron. 15:16)
9. In the ___ was the Word. (John 1:1)
10. Voltage's abbreviation.
11. Ye ___ men with burdens grievous to be borne. (Luke 11:46)
19. Have a ___ and sleep if you want to. (Prov. 24:33, GNB)
20. They see Jesus walking on the ___. (John 6:19)
22. And ___, and Eshtemoh, and Anim. (Josh. 15:50)

23. The things which must shortly be ___. (Rev. 22:6)
24. His ___ [2 words] shall be put to death. (Exod. 21:29)
26. Siamese twin Chang's brother.
29. I am carnal, sold under ___. (Rom. 7:14)
31. The burning ___, that shall consume the eyes, and cause sorrow of heart. (Lev. 26:16)
32. The stone is heavy, and the ___ weighty. (Prov. 27:3)
34. Mrs. Gynt.
36. These are my ___ that my lovers have given me. (Hos. 2:12)
39. Pay her back even as she ___ paid. (Rev. 18:6, ASV)
41. To ___, that God was in Christ. (2 Cor. 5:19)

44. Thou shalt not ___ to offer the first of thy ripe fruits. (Exod. 22:29)
46. Ask me ___ so much dowry and gift. (Gen. 34:12)
47. I saw as it were ___ [2 words] of glass. (Rev. 15:2)
48. Its slave girls ___ like doves. (Nah. 2:7, NIV)
50. Unclothed.
52. To make the cities of Judah desolate, and a ___ of dragons. (Jer. 10:22)
55. How long will it be ___ thou be quiet? (Jer. 47:6)
56. Brought him to an ___, and took care of him. (Luke 10:34)
57. He ___ them out as far as to Bethany. (Luke 24:50)

31

Across

1. That ye may ___ the flesh of kings. (Rev. 19:18)
4. Be baptized, and ___ away thy sins. (Acts 22:16)
8. To make an impression.
12. An ___, and the rain doth nourish it. (Isa. 44:14)
13. Dolphin genus.
14. ___, a prophetess, the daughter of Phanuel. (Luke 2:36)
15. Let me not ___ the death of the child. (Gen. 21:16)
16. If no one comes to rescue us, we will ___ to you. (1 Sam. 11:3, NIV)
18. Ye shall ___ down the wicked. (Mal. 4:3)
20. Rab- ___, with all the residue of the princes of the king of Babylon. (Jer. 39:3)
21. I will put my hook in thy ___. (2 Kings 19:28)
24. Tears.
28. The suckling child shall play on the hole of the ___. (Isa. 11:8)
31. The Spirit of the LORD began to ___ him. (Judg. 13:25)
33. That anointing is ___, not counterfeit. (1 John 2:27, NIV)
34. A poor man is better than a ___. (Prov. 19:22)
36. The first came out ___, all over. (Gen. 25:25)
37. Fully indulge.
38. ___ obeyed Abraham, calling him lord. (1 Peter 3:6)
39. Work units.
41. ___ the tree down, and destroy it. (Dan. 4:23)
42. I am Alpha and ___, the first and the last. (Rev. 1:11)
44. They shall ___ as lions' whelps. (Jer. 51:38)
46. Direction: Jerusalem to Jericho [15 miles].
48. ___ souls were saved by water. (1 Peter 3:20)
52. ___ [3 words] hundred chariots of iron. (Judg. 4:3)
57. The sun and the ___ were darkened. (Rev. 9:2)
58. Danish measure.
59. My doctrine shall ___ as the rain. (Deut. 32:2)
60. Why make ye this ___, and weep? (Mark 5:39)
61. I will put my laws into their ___. (Heb. 8:10)
62. He will be a spirit of justice to him who ___ in judgment. (Isa. 28:6, NIV)
63. But if ye be ___ of the Spirit, ye are not under the law. (Gal. 5:18)

Down

1. The ___ wind brought the locusts. (Exod. 10:13)
2. Phanuel, of the tribe of ___. (Luke 2:36)
3. When thou wast under the fig tree, I saw ___. (John 1:48)
4. Whom I have filled with the spirit of ___. (Exod. 28:3)
5. Babylonian god.
6. ___, thou hast nothing to draw with. (John 4:11)
7. There was no ___ in the pot. (2 Kings 4:41)
8. When men are afraid of heights and of ___ in the streets. (Eccles. 12:5, NIV)
9. For Christ is the ___ of the law. (Rom. 10:4)
10. Direction: Jerusalem to Damascus [140 miles].
11. The Valley of Siddim was full of ___ pits. (Gen. 14:10, NIV)
17. Neither his ___ heavy, that it cannot hear. (Isa. 59:1)
19. This is a deceiver and ___ antichrist. (2 John 7)
22. She weepeth ___ in the night. (Lam. 1:2)
23. They were judged ___ man according to their work. (Rev. 20:13)

25. Goeth out to Remmon-methoar to ___. (Josh. 19:13)
26. He went to the temple to give notice of the ___ when the days of purification would end. (Acts 21:26, NIV)
27. Sin . . . deceived me, and by it ___ me. (Rom. 7:11)
28. I John, who ___ am your brother. (Rev. 1:9)
29. Old Thailand.
30. Shave her head, and ___ her nails. (Deut. 21:12)
32. The children's teeth are set on ___. (Ezek. 18:2)
35. Why do the heathen ___ [2 words] the people imagine a vain thing? (Ps. 2:1)
40. Lord, if he ___, he will get better. (John 11:12, NIV)

43. If we confess our sins, he is faithful ___ just to forgive us. (1 John 1:9)
45. Fifty-one (Roman numerals).
47. All the ___ of the earth shall fear him. (Ps. 67:7)
49. ___ the son of Ebed said, Who is Abimelech? (Judg. 9:28)
50. There is no secret that they can ___ from thee. (Ezek. 28:3)
51. Will you keep to the old path that evil men have ___? (Job 22:15, NIV)
52. ___ is the father of Caanan. (Gen. 9:18)
53. ___ thought she had been drunken. (1 Sam. 1:13)
54. Even as a ___ gathereth her chickens. (Matt. 23:37)
55. Ezbon, and Uzzi and Uzziel, and Jerimoth, and ___. (1 Chron. 7:7)
56. These speak evil of those things which they know ___ (Jude 10)

32

Across

1. ___ begat Nimrod, he began to be mighty upon the earth. (1 Chron. 1:10)
5. The woman went her way, and did eat, and her countenance was no more ___. (1 Sam. 1:18)
8. Protect me from men of violence who plan to ___ my feet. (Ps. 140:4, NIV)
12. Whom all ___ and the world worshippeth. (Acts 19:27)
13. Time period.
14. Where are the gods of Sepharvaim, ___, and Ivah? (2 Kings 18:34)
15. ___ with me a little in my folly. (2 Cor. 11:1)
16. Gold coin.
17. Wherein shall go no galley with ___. (Isa. 33:21)
18. ___ in the valley of decision. (Joel 3:14)
21. They behold your ___ conversation. (1 Peter 3:2)
24. Why should this dead ___ curse my lord? (2 Sam. 16:9)
25. Shamed, who built Ono, and ___. (1 Chron. 8:12)
26. Wayfaring men, though fools, shall not ___ therein. (Isa. 35:8)
28. I commend unto you ___ our sister. (Rom. 16:1)
32. Came the navy of Tarshish, bringing gold, and silver, ivory, and ___, and peacocks. (1 Kings 10:22)
34. Naval distress signal.
36. It ___ them like dirt in the streets. (2 Sam. 22:43, NKJ)
37. Whose waters cast up mire and ___. (Isa. 57:20)
39. Military address.
41. Federal purchasing agency.
42. Doth not the ___ try words? (Job 12:11)
44. Thou shalt observe to do according to all that they ___ thee. (Deut. 17:10)
46. The ___ came to him, and said unto him, What meanest thou, O sleeper? (Jonah 1:6)
50. Hebrew letter (see Ps. 119:65).
51. And their flocks to ___ thunderbolts. (Ps. 78:48)
52. Despise not one of these little ___. (Matt. 18:10)
56. Confederate General Robert ___ ___.
57. Follow peace with ___ men. (Heb. 12:14)
58. Silver and gold have I ___. (Acts 3:6)
59. Woe to those who ___ iniquity. (Mic. 2:1, NIV)
60. The ___ that is in the land of Assyria. (Isa. 7:18)
61. Who his own self bare our sins in his own body on the ___. (1 Peter 2:24)

Down

1. The fourth part of a ___ of dove's dung. (2 Kings 6:25)
2. ___ a little wine for thy stomach's sake. (1 Tim. 5:23)
3. The children of ___, the children of Padon. (Neh. 7:47)
4. Whoever fails to find me ___ himself. (Prov. 8:36, NIV)
5. So the merchants and ___ of all kind of ware lodged without Jerusalem. (Neh. 13:20)
6. Tally up your total.
7. Thou son of ___, have mercy upon me. (Mark 10:48)
8. Take no ___ for your life. (Luke 12:22)
9. Have ye never ___ what David did? (Mark 2:25)
10. Concerning.
11. Heaven and earth shall ___ away. (Mark 13:31)
19. Shoshonean Indian.
20. The ___ of Carmel shall wither. (Amos 1:2)

21. And was ___ with zeal as a cloke. (Isa. 59:17)
22. Pueblo Indian.
23. Zebadiah, and Arad, and ___. (1 Chron. 8:15)
27. Brown kiwi.
29. Therefore!
30. The ___ out of the wood doth waste it. (Ps. 80:13)
31. I am faint: therefore was his name called ___. (Gen. 25:30)
33. They stoned ___, calling upon God. (Acts 7:59)
35. Nor let me alone till I swallow down my ___? (Job 7:19)
38. The sons of ___; Cush, and Mizraim, and Phut, and Canaan. (Gen. 10:6)
40. A tree to be desired to make ___ wise. (Gen. 3:6)

43. Was not ___ the harlot justified by works? (James 2:25)
45. Joab saw that the ___ of the battle was against him. (2 Sam. 10:9)
46. There is but a ___ between me and death. (1 Sam. 20:3)
47. Her house is the way to ___. (Prov. 7:27)
48. Flowering willow.
49. Boils from the ___ of his foot unto his crown. (Job 2:7)
53. Commanded them not to speak at all ___ teach in the name of Jesus. (Acts 4:18)
54. Direction: Nazareth to Tiberias [15 miles].
55. I ___ another law in my members. (Rom. 7:23)

67

33

Across

1. Repent, or ___ I will come unto thee quickly. (Rev. 2:16)
5. They smote him on the head with a ___. (Mark 15:19)
9. He wrote the dream, and told the ___ of the matters. (Dan. 7:1)
12. Hemispherical hammer end.
13. Oil (comb. form).
14. The flesh was yet between their teeth, ___ it was chewed. (Num. 11:33)
15. An ___ well-expressed is like a design of gold, set in silver. (Prov. 25:11, GNB)
16. Thy name is as ___ poured forth. (Song of Sol. 1:3)
18. Wherever there is a ___, there the vultures will gather. (Matt. 24:28, NIV)
20. ___, and he smelleth the battle afar off. (Job 39:25)
21. Truly ___ all the increase of thy seed. (Deut. 14:22)
23. He went to the temple to give notice of the ___. (Acts 21:26, NIV)
27. Thou hast ___ them which say they are apostles. (Rev. 2:2)
30. Ye shall not ___ unto the word. (Deut. 4:2)
32. The glory of God ___ lighten it. (Rev. 21:23)
33. So will we ___ the calves of our lips. (Hos. 14:2)
35. ___ lest any man spoil you through philosophy. (Col. 2:8)
37. There was no room for them in the ___. (Luke 2:7)
38. How is the gold become ___! (Lam. 4:1)
40. Digger for ores.
41. If she ___ the flower of her age. (1 Cor. 7:36)
43. He poured water into a ___, and began to wash the disciples' feet. (John 13:5)
45 ___ hath made him to be sin for us. (2 Cor. 5:21)
47. So Jonah arose, and went unto ___. (Jonah 3:3)
51. They ran out of the house naked and ___. (Acts 19:16, NIV)
55. We all do ___ as a leaf. (Isa. 64:6)
56. ___ for light, spices for anointing. (Exod. 25:6)
57. Ram the firstborn, and Bunah, and ___. (1 Chron. 2:25)
58. The daughter of Phanuel, of the tribe of ___. (Luke 2:36)
59. To take a mate.
60. Paul stood in the midst of ___ hill. (Acts 17:22)
61. The diligent ___ only to plenteousness. (Prov. 21:5)

Down

1. Grand lyric poem.
2. Mother of Castor and Pollux.
3. O thou ___, go, flee thee away into the land of Judah. (Amos 7:12)
4. A better covenant, which has been ___ on better promises. (Heb. 8:6, ASV)
5. The screech owl will ___ in her columns. (Zeph. 2:14, NIV)
6. ___ said, I pray thee, let a double portion of thy spirit be upon me. (2 Kings 2:9)
7. Yet (poetic).
8. Whosoever is born of God ___ not commit sin. (1 John 3:9)
9. ___ that none render evil for evil. (1 Thess. 5:15)
10. Footed vase.
11. A certain damsel possessed with a spirit of divination ___ us. (Acts 16:16)
17. Much learning doth make thee ___. (Acts 26:24)
19. The men of Shechem, which ___ him in the killing of his brethren. (Judg. 9:24)
22. Novelist Bowen's initials.
24. The word that came to Jeremiah from the LORD, after that Nebuzar-___ the captain of the guard had let him go. (Jer. 40:1)

68

25. Never ___ of doing what is right. (2 Thess. 3:13, NIV)
26. Mahli, and ___, and Jeremoth, three. (1 Chron. 23:23)
27. Protect me from men of violence who plan to ___ my feet. (Ps. 140:4, NIV)
28. California rockfish.
29. They came to meet us as far as Appii Forum and Three ___. (Acts 28:15, NKJ)
31. Can a ___ open the eyes of the blind? (John 10:21, NIV)
34. And the ___ . . . made he a woman. (Gen. 2:22)
36. Digged a place for the ___, and built a tower. (Mark 12:1)
39. Be ye holy in all ___ of conversation. (1 Peter 1:15)

42. Notwithstanding ___ shall be saved in childbearing. (1 Tim. 2:15)
44. Confirming the word with ___ following. (Mark 16:20)
46. Esau is ___. (Gen. 36:8)
48. It is worth more than gold, than a gold ___ or finest glass. (Job 28:17, GNB)
49. ___ the garden of God. (Ezek. 28:13)
50. The ___ ran violently down a steep place. (Luke 8:33)
51. At the name of Jesus every knee should ___. (Phil. 2:10)
52. It was impossible for God to ___. (Heb. 6:18)
53. Long ago.
54. ___ the son of Ikkesh the Tekoite. (2 Sam. 23:26)

69

34

Across

1. Find grace to ___ in time of need. (Heb. 4:16)
5. ___, our eye hath seen it. (Ps. 35:21)
8. The Angel which redeemed me from all evil, bless the ___. (Gen. 48:16)
12. They settled in the ___ from Aroer to Nebo. (1 Chron. 5:8, NIV)
13. ___ not the poor, because he is poor. (Prov. 22:22)
14. Mine entrance.
15. The roebuck, and the fallow ___. (Deut. 14:5)
16. They do alway ___ in their heart. (Heb. 3:10)
17. His ___ is called The Word of God. (Rev. 19:13)
18. Jephunneh, and Pispah, and ___. (1 Chron. 7:38)
20. Philip cometh and telleth ___. (John 12:22)
22. Whoever ___ in Him does not sin. (1 John 3:6, NKJ)
25. To any hill which could be dug with a ___, you will not go there. (Isa. 7:25, NKJ)
26. Unto thy word shall all my people be ___. (Gen. 41:40)
27. He who ___ his heart falls into trouble. (Prov. 28:14, NIV)
31. ___ the Ithrite, Gareb the Ithrite. (1 Chron. 11:40)
32. The eyes of them that see shall not be ___. (Isa. 32:3)
33. Ye shall seek me, and shall ___ in your sins. (John 8:21)
34. To have made holes.
37. Jesus saw that a crowd was running to the ___. (Mark 9:25, NIV)
39. Her ___ is to be devoted to the Lord. (1 Cor. 7:34, NIV)
40. More cruel.
41. By faith they passed through the ___ [2 words]. (Heb. 11:29)
44. Rise, Peter; kill and ___. (Acts 11:7)

45. To have landed upon.
46. The kingdom of heaven is like unto a ___. (Matt. 13:47)
48. He ___ the chains apart and broke the irons on his feet. (Mark 5:4, NIV)
52. Anterior.
53. To color.
54. A poor man is better than a ___. (Prov. 19:22)
55. Ye shall find a colt ___, whereon never man sat. (Mark 11:2)
56. But (Latin).
57. Poplars and ___, because the shadow thereof is good. (Hos. 4:13)

Down

1. Nay, I ___ not known sin, but by the law. (Rom. 7:7)
2. Sir, come down ___ my child die. (John 4:49)
3. We sailed to the ___ of Crete, opposite Salmone. (Acts 27:7, NIV)
4. They ___ their sin like Sodom. (Isa. 3:9, NIV)
5. You may set up your own market ___. (1 Kings 20:34, NIV)
6. Aaron thy brother died in mount ___. (Deut. 32:50)
7. ___ fell upon his face, and laughed. (Gen. 17:17)
8. And sailed into Syria, and ___ at Tyre. (Acts 21:3)
9. Went up to ___, and fetched a compass. (Josh. 15:3)
10. American coin.
11. Jacob gave Esau some bread and some lentil ___. (Gen. 25:34, NIV)
19. It will be fair weather: for the sky is ___. (Matt. 16:2)
21. The vile person shall be no more called liberal, ___ the churl said to be bountiful. (Isa. 32:5)
22. It goes through ___ places seeking rest, and does not find it. (Matt. 12:43, NIV)
23. Barbed seed pod.

24. Sibbecai the Hushathite, __ the Ahohite. (1 Chron. 11:29)

27. Adam and his wife ___ themselves. (Gen. 3:8)

28. Thou hast been in ___, the garden of God. (Ezek. 28:13)

29. Were there not ten cleansed? but where are the ___? (Luke 17:17)

30. A Prophet was beforetime called a ___. (1 Sam. 9:9)

32. The ruler ___ gifts, the judge accepts bribes. (Micah 7:3, NIV)

35. She wept before him the seven days, while their feast ___. (Judg. 14:17)

36. It was impossible for God to ___. (Heb. 6:18)

37. They see Jesus walking on the ___. (John 6:19)

38. Abram was very rich in ___. (Gen. 13:2)

40. Who hath . . . ___ out heaven with the span. (Isa. 40:12)

41. Floating platform.

42. ___, lama sabachthani? (Mark 15:34)

43. A ___ vision has been shown to me. (Isa. 21:2, NIV)

47. He cometh with clouds; and every ___ shall see him. (Rev. 1:7)

49. My head with ___ thou didst not anoint. (Luke 7:46)

50. Behind him a ___ caught in a thicket by his horns. (Gen. 22:13)

51. Bitter vetch.

35

Across

1. Mattathias, which was the son of ___. (Luke 3:25)
5. ___ was not deceived. (1 Tim. 2:14)
9. The ___ which thou sawest having two horns. (Dan. 8:20)
12. Pail (Latin).
13. Moses made a serpent of brass, and put it upon a ___. (Num. 21:9)
14. Direction: Emmaus to Bethany [6 miles].
15. ___, and Dumah, and Eshean. (Josh. 15:52)
16. Neither do the ___ understand. (Job 32:9)
17. ___ shall be a serpent by the way. (Gen. 49:17)
18. Take thee a ___ razor, and cause it to pass upon thine head. (Ezek. 5:1)
20. Out of whose womb came the ___? (Job 38:29)
22. Go to the ___, thou sluggard. (Prov. 6:6)
23. All they that cast angle into the brooks shall ___. (Isa. 19:8)
26. Divine Comedy author.
29. Ye have made it a ___ of thieves. (Mark 11:17)
30. Indian tree.
31. American state.
32. Take up thy ___, and walk. (John 5:8)
33. Bill's soft spot.
34. S. African hill.
35. A time to rend, and a time to ___. (Eccles. 3:7)
36. The great city, which spiritually is called ___ and Egypt. (Rev. 11:8)
37. Zabad begat ___. (1 Chron. 2:37)
39. Besought him that they might only touch the ___ of his garment. (Matt. 14:36)
40. They are extinct, they are quenched as ___. (Isa. 43:17)
41. He made the ___ and the wall to lament. (Lam. 2:8)

45. Pagoda.
47. The children of Shem; ___, and Ashur. (Gen. 10:22)
49. To the sheltered side.
50. See thou hurt not the ___ and the wine. (Rev. 6:6)
51. Chinese (comb. form).
52. Estonian weight.
53. The man said unto ___, I am he that came out of the army. (1 Sam. 4:16)
54. The sword to slay, and the dogs to ___. (Jer. 15:3)
55. They shall ___ as lions' whelps. (Jer. 51:38)

Down

1. Elijah said unto ___, Get thee up, eat and drink. (1 Kings 18:41)
2. Call me not Naomi, call me ___. (Ruth 1:20)
3. The sons of Eliphaz; Teman, and ___. (1 Chron. 1:36)
4. Remember the ___ day, to keep it holy. (Exod. 20:8)
5. Wherefore lay ___ all filthiness. (James 1:21)
6. The ___ came and licked his sores. (Luke 16:21)
7. Bitter beer.
8. Darius the ___ took the kingdom. (Dan. 5:31)
9. The Angel which ___ me from all evil. (Gen. 48:16)
10. She had made an idol in a grove; and ___ destroyed her idol. (1 Kings 15:13)
11. Follow peace with all ___, and holiness. (Heb. 12:14)
19. Direction: Nazareth to Tiberias [15 miles].
21. 900 [Roman numerals].
23. If ye be ___ of the Spirit, ye are not under the law. (Gal. 5:18)
24. When Paul was brought before ___. (2 Tim. subscript)

25. The Nile will ___ with frogs. (Exod. 8:3, NIV)
26. The sons of Eliphaz the firstborn son of Esau: ___ Teman. (Gen. 36:15)
27. At the top.
28. The sons of ___; Jahzeel, and Guni. (Gen. 46:24)
29. God give thee of the ___ of heaven. (Gen. 27:28)
32. Babylon is taken, ___ is confounded. (Jer. 50:2)
33. Make them sit down by fifties in a ___. (Luke 9:14)
35. Be not afraid: for what ___ thou? (1 Sam. 28:13)
36. ___, which was the son of Noe. (Luke 3:36)

38. ___, I come to do thy will, O God. (Heb. 10:9)
39. A parcel of ground which Jacob bought of the sons of ___. (Josh. 24:32)
41. There ___ [2 words] young man, and told Moses. (Num. 11:27)
42. Wing-like.
43. The earth shall ___ to and fro like a drunkard. (Isa. 24:20)
44. I will ___ thee the mystery of the woman. (Rev. 17:7)
45. Upon the great ___ of their right foot. (Exod. 29:20)
46. To feel uneasy.
48. Hath Satan filled thine heart to ___ to the Holy Ghost? (Acts 5:3)

36

Across

1. Covet earnestly the ___ gifts. (1 Cor. 12:31)
5. Lot.
9. Their bows will ___ down the young men. (Isa. 13:18, ASV)
12. ___ the father of Hushah. (1 Chron. 4:4)
13. Begat a son in his own likeness, after his image; and called his name ___. (Gen. 5:3)
14. Pochereth of Zebaim, the children of ___. (Ezra 2:57)
15. The children shouting in the temple ___. (Matt. 21:15, NIV)
16. Shammah the son of ___. (2 Sam. 23:11)
17. Cleave.
18. Before all thy people I will do ___. (Exod. 34:10)
20. The great day of his ___ has come. (Rev. 6:17)
22. Shade tree.
23. Raging waves of the ___, foaming out their own shame. (Jude 13)
24. He ___ but the pain of his own body. (Job 14:22, NIV)
27. She turned herself, and saith unto him, ___. (John 20:16)
31. ___ yourselves likewise with the same mind. (1 Peter 4:1)
32. To ___, that God was in Christ. (2 Cor. 5:19)
33. Do ___ err, my beloved brethren. (James 1:16)
34. The holy women also, who ___ in God. (1 Peter 3:5)
37. The LORD God make coats of ___, and clothed them. (Gen. 3:21)
39. Who ___ thou that judgest another man's servant? (Rom. 14:4)
40. ___ that none render evil for evil. (1 Thess. 5:15)
41. The fathers have eaten a sour ___. (Jer. 31:29)
44. He saw a man, named ___, sitting at the receipt of custom. (Matt. 9:9)

48. All that handle the ___, the mariners. (Ezek. 27:29)
49. Reckon.
51. We spend our years as a ___ that is told. (Ps. 90:9)
52. The ___ of violence is in their hands. (Isa. 59:6)
53. Bind the ___ of thine head upon thee. (Ezek. 24:17)
54. Elizabeth derivative.
55. German article.
56. Jesus Christ of the ___ of David. (2 Tim. 2:8)
57. Of ___, the family of the Eranites. (Num. 26:36)

Down

1. Cast out the ___ out of thine own eye. (Matt. 7:5)
2. ___ the scribe stood upon a pulpit of wood. (Neh. 8:4)
3. The LORD came unto Gad, David's ___. (2 Sam. 24:11)
4. But who was also chosen of the churches to ___ with us with this grace. (2 Cor. 8:19)
5. Every one of you hath a ___. (1 Cor. 14:26)
6. He was dead already, they brake not his ___. (John 19:33)
7. I ___ no pleasant bread. (Dan. 10:3)
8. If thou weavest the seven locks of my head with ___ [2 words]. (Judg. 16:13)
9. Call me not Naomi, call me ___. (Ruth 1:20)
10. I command you; do not ___ a word. (Jer. 26:2, NIV)
11. The Lord cometh ___ ten thousands of his saints. (Jude 14)
19. Otherwise (Scottish).
21. God will hear all the words of ___ - shakeh. (2 Kings 19:4)
23. As of fire, and it ___ upon each of them. (Acts 2:3)
24. Let them not fail to burn the ___. (1 Sam. 2:16)

25. Do they not ___ that devise evil? (Prov. 14:22)
26. Big bird of Australia.
27. I will ___ you out of their bondage. (Exod. 6:6)
28. She called his name Ben- ___; but his father called him Benjamin. (Gen. 35:18)
29. ___ his son, Jehoshuah his son. (1 Chron. 7:27)
30. That which groweth of ___ own accord. (Lev. 25:5)
32. His body was ___ with the dew. (Dan. 4:33)
35. The trees of the LORD are full of ___. (Ps. 104:16)
36. She ___ her young harshly. (Job 39:16, NIV)
37. Our brother Timothy is ___ at liberty. (Heb. 13:23)

38. He struck it into the pan, or ___. (1 Sam. 2:14)
40. He has filled me with bitter herbs and ___ me with gall. (Lam. 3:15, NIV)
41. Slew of the Philistines six hundred men with an ox ___. (Judg. 3:31)
42. Whosoever shall say to his brother, ___, shall be in the danger of the council. (Matt. 5:22)
43. Many of them also which used curious ___. (Acts 19:19)
44. But ___ talk leads only to poverty. (Prov. 14:23, ASV)
45. John had his raiment of camel's ___. (Mark 1:6)
46. "Born Free" lioness.
47. To break a habit gradually.
50. The wheat and the ___ were not smitten. (Exod. 9:32)

37

Across

1. ___ thought she had been drunken. (1 Sam. 1:13)
4. Agile.
8. Enos, which was the son of ___. (Luke 3:38)
12. The land of ___, on the east of Eden. (Gen. 4:16)
13. Barge [French].
14. Shallowest Great Lake.
15. The Father, the Word, and the Holy Ghost: and these three are ___. (1 John 5:7)
16. Thou shalt not approach to his wife: she is thine ___. (Lev. 18:14)
17. Shave her head, and ___ her nails. (Deut. 21:12)
18. My back is filled with ___ pain. (Ps. 38:7, NIV)
20. He has filled me with bitter herbs and ___ me with gall. (Lam. 3:15, NIV)
21. The ___ of all things is at hand. (1 Peter 4:7)
22. For ye shall speak into the ___. (1 Cor. 14:9)
23. He ___ to be a proclaimer of strange deities. (Acts 17:18, ASV)
26. The children of Reuben, ___ eldest son. (Num. 1:20)
30. Roof edge.
31. Make thee an ___ of gopher wood. (Gen. 6:14)
32. Cursed is every one that hangeth on a ___. (Gal. 3:13)
33. The devils also believe, and ___. (James 2:19)
35. ___ gave Solomon cedar trees and fir trees. (1 Kings 5:10)
36. I will punish ___ in Babylon. (Jer. 51:44)
37. In all things ye are ___ superstitious. (Acts 17:22)
38. Hewed stones, ___ with saws, within and without. (1 Kings 7:9)
41. In the name of our God we will set up our ___. (Ps. 20:5)
45. For this ___ is Mount Sinai. (Gal. 4:25)
46. Call the poor, the maimed, the ___, the blind. (Luke 14:13)
47. Hath Satan filled thine heart to ___ to the Holy Ghost? (Acts 5:3)
48. Certain men crept in unawares, who ___ before of old ordained to this condemnation. (Jude 4)
49. Nevertheless ___ heart was perfect. (1 Kings 15:14)
50. I took the little book out of the angel's hand, and ___ it up. (Rev. 10:10)
51. God shall ___ them strong delusion. (2 Thess. 2:11)
52. I would thou ___ cold or hot. (Rev. 3:15)
53. The tabernacle of God is with ___. (Rev. 21:3)

Down

1. ___, which was the son of Seth. (Luke 3:38)
2. Seeing a ___ fig tree by the road. (Matt. 21:19, ASV)
3. Their ___ of pleasure is to carouse. (2 Peter 2:13, NIV)
4. They are ___ and blemishes, reveling in their deceptions. (2 Peter 2:13, ASV)
5. A mixture of myrrh and aloes, about an hundred ___ weight. (John 19:39)
6. Ladder step.
7. Ye have not ___ resisted unto blood. (Heb. 12:4)
8. All the days of his ___ shall he eat nothing. (Num. 6:4)
9. He was [Latin].
10. Never ___ of doing what is right. (2 Thess. 3:13, NIV)
11. Ye do well that ye take ___. (2 Peter 1:19)
19. God hath ___ her iniquities. (Rev. 18:5)
20. ___, thou hast nothing to draw with. (John 4:11)

22. Whatsoever we ___, we receive. (1 John 3:22)
23. I have ___ before thee an open door. (Rev. 3:8)
24. What ye hear in the ___, that preach ye upon the housetops. (Matt. 10:27)
25. Adam called his wife's name ___. (Gen. 3:20)
26. Wrath.
27. The spirit of whoredoms hath caused them to ___. (Hos. 4:12)
28. Pasture.
29. ___, which was the son of Noe. (Luke 3:36)
31. To God the Judge of ___. (Heb. 12:23)
34. Aeneas, which had kept his ___. (Acts 9:33)

35. Providing for ___ things, not only in the sight of the Lord. (2 Cor. 8:21)
37. I love ___, my brother Absalom's sister. (2 Sam. 23:11)
38. Cut them with ___, and with harrows of iron. (1 Chron. 20:3)
39. Shammah the son of ___. (2 Sam. 13:4)
40. But as my beloved sons I ___ you. (1 Cor. 4:14)
41. Who in presence am ___ among you. (2 Cor. 10:1)
42. Behold, I will break the bow of ___. (Jer. 49:35)
43. He must do so according to the ___ of Passover. (Num. 9:14, NKJ)
44. He that doeth evil hath not ___ God. (3 John 11)
46. Sin is the transgression of the ___. (1 John 3:4)

77

38

Across

1. Every one could sling stones at an hair breadth, and not ___. (Judg. 20:16)
5. The sceptre from the house of ___. (Amos 1:5)
9. For ___ hath been a succourer of many. (Rom. 16:2)
12. And withal they learn to be ___. (1 Tim. 5:13)
13. Thy ___ is as the tower of Lebanon. (Song of Sol. 7:4)
14. Take heed therefore ___ ye hear. (Luke 8:18)
15. Tidy.
16. ___ the first, Obadiah the second. (1 Chron. 12:9)
17. Ye have an unction from the Holy ___. (1 John 2:20)
18. They meet with darkness in the ___. (Job 5:14)
20. The ___ of hell shall not prevail against it. (Matt. 16:18)
22. I ___ in Sion a chief corner stone. (1 Peter 2:6)
23. Coated it with ___ and pitch. (Exod. 2:3, NIV)
24. Melchisedec king of ___. (Heb. 7:1)
27. A painful physical ___, which acts as Satan's messenger. (2 Cor. 12:7, GNB)
31. Cornelius said, Four days ___ I was fasting. (Acts 10:30)
32. Child shall play on the hole of the ___. (Isa. 11:8)
33. By grace ye ___ saved. (Eph. 2:5)
34. The LORD ___ all the proud of heart. (Prov. 16:5, NIV)
37. Solomon gave ___ twenty thousand measures of wheat for food. (1 Kings 5:11)
39. Deliver thyself as a ___ from the hand of the hunter. (Prov. 6:5)
40. Little children, ___ no man deceive you. (1 John 3:7)
41. Ye shall be ___ of all men for my name's sake. (Luke 21:17)
44. Happy is he that condemneth not ___. (Rom. 14:22)
48. They do alway ___ in their heart. (Heb. 3:10)
49. Ram the firstborn, and Bunah, and ___. (1 Chron. 2:25)
51. God cannot be tempted with ___. (James 1:13)
52. The wheat and the ___ was not smitten. (Exod. 9:32)
53. I liken you, my darling, to a ___. (Song of Sol. 1:9, NIV)
54. Matthat, which was the son of ___. (Luke 3:24)
55. Lyric poem.
56. I am alive for evermore, ___. (Rev. 1:18)
57. ___ not thyself because of evil men. (Prov. 24:19)

Down

1. I will put my laws into their ___. (Heb. 8:10)
2. He had no ___ that what the angel was doing was really happening. (Acts 12:9, NIV)
3. Arise, Peter; ___ and eat. (Acts 11:7)
4. Make you perfect, stablish, strengthen, ___ you. (1 Peter 5:10)
5. A friend of the world is the ___ of God. (James 4:4)
6. They never ___ or sleep. (Isa. 5:27, GNB)
7. Direction: Jerusalem to Bethany [2.5 miles]
8. The men of Cuth made ___. (2 Kings 17:30)
9. It was as though it budded, and her blossoms ___ forth. (Gen. 40:10)
10. Whetstone.
11. From following the ___ great with young he brought him to feed Jacob. (Ps. 78:71)
19. Because I said, ___ [2 words] the Son of God. (John 10:36)
21. ___ yourselves likewise with the same mind. (1 Peter 4:1)
23. He may dip the ___ of his finger in water. (Luke 16:24)
24. One to another, as ye walk, and are ___? (Luke 24:17)

25. We know not; he is of ___; ask him. (John 9:21)
26. The ___ fell upon Matthias. (Acts 1:26)
27. Who hath sent out the wild ___ free? (Job 39:5)
28. His kinsman whose ___ Peter cut off. (John 18:26)
29. "Blue Eagle."
30. Egyptian god of the setting sun.
32. And ___ the sacrifices of the dead. (Ps. 106:28)
35. How long will it be ___ thou be quiet? (Jer. 47:6)
36. We had been as ___, and been made like unto Gomorrha. (Rom. 9:29)
37. Came behind him, and touched the ___ of his garment. (Matt. 9:20)

38. Of the truth ___: yea, and we also bear record. (3 John 12)
40. The ___ clothes laid by themselves. (Luke 24:12)
41. When the Philistines saw that their ___ was dead. (1 Sam. 17:51, NIV)
42. It goes through ___ places seeking rest. (Matt. 12:43, NIV)
43. I give to eat of the ___ of life. (Rev. 2:7)
44. The time of your sojourning ___ in fear. (1 Peter 1:17)
45. ___ learning, and never able to come to the knowledge of the truth. (2 Tim. 3:7)
46. ___ according to God in the spirit. (1 Peter 4:6)
47. To fly lightly.
50. Elihu the son of Barachel the Buzite, of the kindred of ___. (Job 32:2)

39

Across

1. They sung as it were a new ___. (Rev. 14:3)
5. Let this mind be in you, which ___ also in Christ Jesus. (Phil. 2:5)
8. Kept not their first estate, but ___ their own habitation. (Jude 6)
12. And the poor for a ___ of shoes. (Amos 2:6)
13. Why make ye this ___, and weep? (Mark 5:39)
14. ___ the Ahohite. (1 Chron. 11:29)
15. The Pharisees began to ___ him vehemently. (Luke 11:53)
16. Blessed be he that enlargeth ___. (Deut. 33:20)
17. I am the ___, ye are the branches. (John 15:5)
18. The sons of ___ his brother were, Ulam his firstborn, Jehush the second. (1 Chron. 8:39)
20. So must thou bear witness also at ___. (Acts 23:11)
22. Sheep disease.
24. Jerusalem which is above is free, which is the ___ of us all. (Gal. 4:26)
28. Ye ask, and ___ not, because ye ask amiss. (James 4:3)
32. Thou art as a ___ in the seas. (Ezek. 32:2)
33. A brother ___ [2 words] sister is not under bondage. (1 Cor. 7:15)
34. Their word will ___ as doth a canker. (2 Tim. 2:17)
36. Danish fjord.
37. What ___ thee, O thou sea? (Ps. 114:5)
40. He blew a trumpet, and they ___ from the city, every man to his tent. (2 Sam. 20:22)
43. The God of the armies of Israel, whom thou hast ___. (1 Sam. 17:45)
45. No striker, ___ given to filthy lucre. (Titus 1:7)
46. They ___ not the bones till the morrow. (Zeph. 3:3)
48. His sister Hammoleketh bare ___. (1 Chron. 7:18)
52. By faith, ___, being warned of God

of things not seen as yet, moved with fear. (Heb. 11:7)
55. Asahel was as light of foot as a wild ___. (2 Sam. 2:18)
57. Take thine ___, eat, drink, and be merry. (Luke 12:19)
58. The lightning cometh out of the ___. (Matt. 24:27)
59. To ___ them that dwell upon the earth. (Rev. 3:10)
60. Though ye have ___ among the pots. (Ps. 68:13)
61. Flat carrying device.
62. They shall ___ his face; and his name shall be in their foreheads. (Rev. 22:4)
63. Frighten.

Down

1. Drink ye, and be drunken, and ___, and fall, and rise no more. (Jer. 25:27)
2. Wherein shall go no galley with ___. (Isa. 33:21)
3. The coming of the Lord draweth___. (James 5:8)
4. He came into ___, and there abode three months. (Acts 20:2–3)
5. Every one that passeth by her shall hiss, and ___ his hand. (Zeph. 2:15)
6. The twelfth month, that is, the month ___. (Esther 3:7)
7. The great city, which spiritually is called ___ and Egypt. (Rev. 11:8)
8. None of us ___ to himself. (Rom. 14:7)
9. Samuel feared to show ___ the vision. (1 Sam. 3:15)
10. Winnowed with the shovel and with the ___. (Isa. 30:24)
11. ___ the kine to the cart. (1 Sam. 6:7)
19. Japanese carp.
21. Their bows will ___ down the young men. (Isa. 13:18, ASV)
23. Adam was first formed, then ___. (1 Tim. 2:13)
25. John had his raiment of camel's ___. (Matt. 3:4)
26. I am God, and there is none ___. (Isa. 45:22)

27. A bruised ___ shall he not break. (Matt. 12:20)
28. Whither have ye made a ___ today? (1 Sam. 27:10)
29. Smallest Great Lake.
30. The second beast like a ___. (Rev. 4:7)
31. First the blade, then the ___. (Mark 4:28)
35. Though ye have ___ thousand instructors in Christ. (1 Cor. 4:15)
38. Lamech lived an hundred ___ and two years and begat a son. (Gen. 5:28)
39. He lieth in wait secretly as a lion in his ___. (Ps. 10:9)
41. Hadadezer had wars with ___. (2 Sam. 8:10)
42. Charity vaunteth not ___. (1 Cor. 13:4)

44. To quench all the fiery ___ of the wicked. (Eph. 6:16)
47. He ___ cursing as his garment. (Ps. 109:18, NIV)
49. ___, thou that art highly favoured. (Luke 1:28)
50. He saith also in ___, I will call them my people, which were not my people. (Rom. 9:25)
51. I will not ___ thee in any wise. (Mark 14:31)
52. At thy word I will let down the ___. (Luke 5:5)
53. All that handle the ___, the mariners. (Ezek. 27:29)
54. There was war between ___ and Baasha. (1 Kings 15:32)
56. It is easier for a camel to go through a needle's ___. (Luke 18:25)

81

40

Across

1. Thou art Simon the son of ___. (John 1:42)
5. There shall be a bridle in the ___ of the people, causing them to err. (Isa. 30:28)
9. It is certain we ___ carry nothing out. (1 Tim. 6:7)
12. Despise not one of these little ___. (Matt. 18:10)
13. Administrative type (abbr.).
14. Tyre and Sidon, they would have repented long ___ in sackcloth and ashes. (Matt. 11:21)
15. David answered and said, Call me ___. (1 Kings 1:28)
17. These are unclean for you: the weasel, the ___, any kind of great lizard. (Lev. 11:29, NIV)
18. Water (French).
19. ___ is neither Jew nor Greek. (Gal. 3:28)
21. We his servants will ___ and build. (Neh. 2:20)
24. He has filled me with bitter herbs and ___ me with gall. (Lam. 3:15, NIV)
26. In the book of the ___ of the LORD. (Num. 21:14)
27. Simeon that was called ___. (Acts 13:1)
28. In whom ___ have redemption through his blood. (Col. 1:4)
30. ___ the Jairite was David's priest. (2 Sam. 20:26, NIV)
31. Passenger ship.
32. That we may have boldness in the ___ of judgment. (1 John 4:17)
33. Be diligent to come unto ___ to Nicopolis. (Titus 3:12)
34. The ___ of mountains is his pasture. (Job 39:8)
35. Ephraim is a ___ not turned. (Hos. 7:8)
36. Saw I none, save ___, the Lord's brother. (Gal. 1:19)
37. O ye dry ___, hear the word of the Lord. (Ezek. 37:4)
38. An end to sin, to ___ for wickedness. (Dan. 9:24, NIV)
40. The ___ sitting upon the young. (Deut. 22:6)
41. They think it strange that ye ___ not with them to the same excess of riot. (1 Peter 4:4)
42. ___, which at the first came to Jesus by night. (John 19:39)
48. Business degree.
49. Things that were commanded of him? I ___ not. (Luke 17:9)
50. The leaves of the ___ were for the healing of the nations. (Rev. 22:2)
51. ___ Lord; yet the dogs under the table eat. (Mark 7:28)
52. Lo, a Lamb stood on the mount ___. (Rev. 14:1)
53. Hide it there in a ___ of the rock. (Jer. 13:4)

Down

1. Ye have heard of the patience of ___. (James 5:11)
2. Cape Horn native.
3. Heaven is like unto a ___, that was cast into the sea. (Matt. 13:47)
4. ___ bread shall be fat. (Gen. 49:20)
5. I will avenge the blood of Jezreel upon the house of ___. (Hos. 1:4)
6. The ___ is laid unto the root of the trees. (Luke 3:9)
7. Whose trust shall be a spider's ___. (Job. 8:14)
8. They came out as a whirlwind to ___ me. (Hab. 3:14)
9. Gallio ___ for none of those things. (Acts 18:17)
10. For this ___ is mount Sinai in Arabia. (Gal. 4:25)
11. ___ that man, and have no company with him. (2 Thess. 3:14)
16. On the morrow I ___ on the judgment seat. (Acts 25:17)
20. The sow that was washed to ___ wallowing. (2 Peter 2:22)
21. Kill the prisoners, lest any of them should ___ out, and escape. (Acts 27:42)
22. The devil threw him down, and ___ him. (Luke 9:42)

23. Jephunneh, and Pispah, and ___. (1 Chron. 7:38)
24. Who ___ songs to a heavy heart. (Prov. 25:20, NIV)
25. Shammah the son of ___ the Hararite. (2 Sam. 23:11)
27. Doth he not leave the ninety and ___? (Matt. 18:12)
28. Whether we ___ or sleep, we should live together with him. (1 Thess. 5:10)
29. Let their ___ be darkened, that they may not see. (Rom. 11:10)
31. My heart ___ for Moab like a flute. (Jer. 48:36, NIV)
32. ___ shall judge his people. (Gen. 49:16)
34. The way of Cain, and ___ greedily after the error of Balaam for reward. (Jude 11)

35. Behold, he ___ with clouds. (Rev. 1:7)
36. They repented at the preaching of ___. (Luke 11:32)
37. Gathered together all as many as they found, both ___ and good. (Matt. 22:10)
38. To make war against him that sat on the horse, and against his ___. (Rev. 19:19)
39. Subway.
40. Casting ___ imaginations. (2 Cor. 10:5)
43. Uzzi and Uzziel, and Jerimoth, and ___. (1 Chron. 7:7)
44. Dove murmur.
45. Indo-Chinese language.
46. The sons of Bani; Maadai, Amram, and ___. (Ezra 10:34)
47. ___ then that ye walk circumspectly. (Eph. 5:15)

41

Across

1. The children of Lod, Hadid, and ___. (Ezra 2:33)
4. Many of them also which used curious ___. (Acts 19:19)
8. Go up, O ___: besiege, O Media. (Isa. 21:2)
12. Lord, are there ___ that be saved? (Luke 13:23)
13. The life is ___ than meat. (Luke 12:23)
14. Web tissue.
15. As a ___ of the Way, which they call a sect. (Acts 24:14, NIV)
17. Reward her ___ as she rewarded you. (Rev. 18:6)
18. Gave him to wife Asenath daughter of Poti-pherah priest of ___. (Gen. 41:45)
19. Greed.
21. They ___ not the bones till the morrow. (Zeph. 3:3)
24. They cast four anchors out of the ___. (Acts 27:29)
25. For the sky is ___ and lowring. (Matt. 16:3)
26. King (Spanish).
27. The fourth beast was like a flying ___. (Rev. 4:7)
31. Agar is mount Sinai in ___. (Gal. 4:25)
33. You lie on beds ___ with ivory. (Amos 6:4, NIV)
34. His feet and ankle ___ received strength. (Acts 3:7)
35. Ancient Biblical weight.
36. He was a thief, and had the ___. (John 12:6)
37. John also was baptizing in ___ near Salim. (John 3:23)
39. The ___, because he cheweth the cud. (Lev. 11:6)
40. Her bowels ___ upon her son. (1 Kings 3:26)
43. ___ of good cheer; I have overcome the world. (John 16:33)

44. Or ___ believe me for the very works' sake. (John 14:11)
45. The barbarians saw the ___ beast hang on his hand. (Acts 28:4)
50. I have suffered the ___ of all things. (Phil. 3:8)
51. Neither at any time ___ we flattering words, as ye know. (1 Thess. 2:5)
52. Uzzi and Uzziel, and Jerimoth, and ___. (1 Chron. 7:7)
53. Record my lament; ___ my tears. (Ps. 56:8, NIV)
54. Who can ___ the bottles of heaven? (Job 38:37)
55. Your lightning ___ up the world. (Ps. 77:18, NIV)

Down

1. Put ___ the old man with his deeds. (Col. 3:9)
2. New (comb. form).
3. I am like an ___ of the desert. (Ps. 102:6)
4. Josiah the son of ___. (Jer. 1:2)
5. The third ___ a ligure, an agate, and an amethyst. (Exod. 28:19)
6. Will he break the ___ and yet escape? (Ezek. 17:15, NIV)
7. Purge your conscience from dead works to ___ the living God. (Heb. 9:14)
8. God hath given to us ___ life. (1 John 2:25)
9. ___ made him a great feast in his own house. (Luke 5:29)
10. Fish sauce.
11. Do you give the horse his strength or clothe his neck with a flowing ___? (Job 39:19, NIV)
16. But condescend to men of ___ estate. (Rom. 12:16)
20. Like men condemned to die in the ___. (1 Cor. 4:9, NIV)
21. To take suddenly.
22. When Paul was brought before ___ (2 Tim. subscr.)

23. Nebuzar-___, captain of the guard, servant of the king of Babylon. (2 Kings 25:8)

24. The ___ gave up the dead which were in it. (Rev. 20:13)

26. If ye then be ___ with Christ, seek those things which are above. (Col. 3:1)

28. The men of Ramah, and ___, six hundred twenty and one. (Neh. 7:30)

29. Who is a ___ but he that denieth . . . Jesus. (1 John 2:22)

30. Etham, in the ___ of the wilderness. (Exod. 13:20)

32. Rejoice, thou barren that ___ not. (Gal. 4:27)

33. There was no room for them in the ___. (Luke 2:7)

35. Thou ___ him a little lower than the angels. (Heb. 2:7)

38. Birthmark.

39. Came behind him, and touched the ___ of his garment. (Matt. 9:20)

40. They shall ___ as lion's whelps. (Jer. 51:38)

41. ___, lama sabacthani? (Mark 15:34)

42. Thy King cometh, sitting on an ___ colt. (John 12:15)

43. He disputed about the ___ of Moses. (Jude 9)

46. Education organization.

47. Give us of your ___; for our lamps are gone out. (Matt. 25:8)

48. Bezaleel the son of ___. (Exod. 31:2)

49. I ___ a queen, and am no widow. (Rev. 18:7)

42

Across

1. Take an ___ and push it through his ear lobe into the door. (Deut. 15:17, NIV)
4. Cribs.
8. I and thou rode together after ___. (2 Kings 9:25)
12. To live is Christ, and to ___ is gain. (Phil. 1:21)
13. Fabulist.
14. Book leaf.
15. The dumb ___ speaking with man's voice. (2 Peter 2:16)
16. ___ hairs are here and there upon him. (Hos. 7:9)
17. The children shouting in the temple ___, "Hosanna to the Son of David." (Matt. 21:15, NIV)
18. To build Jerusalem unto the ___. (Dan. 9:25)
20. When a strong man ___ keepeth his palace. (Luke 11:21)
21. The Father, the Word, and the Holy Ghost: and these three are ___. (1 John 5:7)
22. Be gentle unto all men, ___ to teach. (2 Tim. 2:24)
23. Lo, a Lamb stood on the mount ___. (Rev. 14:1)
26. He that hath the Son hath ___. (1 John 5:12)
28. The way a ___ cutter engraves a seal. (Exod. 28:11, NIV)
31. ___, lama sabachthani? that is to say, My God, my God, why hast thou forsaken me? (Matt. 27:46)
32. Springs without water and ___ driven by a storm. (2 Peter 2:17, NIV)
33. ___ ye come out as against a thief? (Matt. 26:55)
34. Casting ___ your care upon him. (1 Peter 5:7)
35. Substitutes suffix.
36. Men's sins are ___ beforehand. (1 Tim. 5:24)
37. For the ___ that is in the land of Assyria. (Isa. 7:18)
38. Eat not of it ___, nor sodden at all with water, but roast with fire. (Exod. 12:9)

40. The ___ in the heaven knoweth her appointed times. (Jer. 8:7)
43. Lot ___ in the cities of the plain. (Gen. 13:12)
47. The labourer is worthy of his ___. (Luke 10:7)
48. Direction (abbr.).
49. ___ had an army of men that bare targets. (2 Chron. 14:8)
50. Their ___ of pleasure is to carouse in broad daylight. (2 Peter 2:13, NIV)
51. Latin initials for Jesus of Nazareth, King of the Jews.
52. They ___ my path, they set forward my calamity. (Job 30:13)
53. To remain undecided.
54. Let them sing aloud upon their ___. (Ps. 149:5)
55. ___ holy men of God spake as they were moved by the Holy Ghost. (2 Peter 1:21)

Down

1. Death reigned from ___ to Moses. (Rom. 5:14)
2. Be not ___ in your own conceits. (Rom. 12:16)
3. The ___ is blessed of the better. (Heb. 7:7)
4. Judgment must ___ at the house of God. (1 Peter 4:17)
5. Behold an ___ indeed, in whom is no guile! (John 1:47)
6. When once the longsuffering of God waited in the days of ___. (1 Peter 3:20)
7. Who came in privily to ___ out our liberty. (Gal. 2:4)
8. Come ye yourselves ___ into a desert place. (Mark 6:31)
9. Do thyself no ___: for we are all here. (Acts 16:28)
10. Shammah the son of ___. (2 Sam. 23:11)
11. Rosary.
19. Is not this the carpenter's ___? (Matt. 13:55)
20. The ships of Tarshish bringing gold, and silver, ivory, and ___, and peacocks. (2 Chron. 9:21)

1	2	3	■	4	5	6	7	■	8	9	10	11
12			■	13				■	14			
15			■	16				■	17			
18			19				■	20				
■	■	■	21			■	22			■	■	■
23	24	25		■	26	27			■	28	29	30
31			■	32				■	33			
34			■	35				■	36			
■	■	■	37			■	38	39		■	■	■
40	41	42		■	43				■	44	45	46
47			■	48				■	49			
50			■	51				■	52			
53			■	54				■	55			

22. The Lord, having saved the people out of the land of Egypt, ___ destroyed them that believed not. (Jude 5)

23. They saw him walking upon the ___. (Mark 6:49)

24. Love worketh no ___ to his neighbour. (Rom. 13:10)

25. See thou hurt not the ___ and the wine. (Rev. 6:6)

27. Adherent.

28. Stand in the ___ before me. (Ezek. 22:30)

29. Sir, come down ___ my child die. (John 4:49)

30. Follow peace with all ___, and holiness. (Heb. 12:14)

32. For I am ___ and lowly in heart. (Matt. 11:29)

36. There shall the great ___ make her nest, and lay, and hatch, and gather under her shadow. (Isa. 34:15)

37. For the ___ of God is he which cometh down. (John 6:33)

39. Patronage.

40. Except these abide in the ___, ye cannot be saved. (Acts 27:31)

41. He hanged on a tree until even ___. (Josh. 8:29)

42. Ram the firstborn, and Bunah, and ___. (1 Chron. 2:25)

43. Jesus saith unto them, Come and ___. (John 21:12)

44. The ___ is the light thereof. (Rev. 21:23)

45. By faith Isaac blessed Jacob and ___. (Heb. 11:20)

46. Till a ___ strike through his liver. (Prov. 7:23)

48. Pool (Scot.).

43

Across

1. Whatsoever goeth upon his ___, . . . those are unclean unto you. (Lev. 11:27)
5. O Lord, which art, and ___, and shalt be. (Rev. 16:5)
9. Wherein was the golden ___ that had manna. (Heb. 9:4)
12. Acidity (comb. form).
13. Tall (Spanish).
14. Why make ye this ___, and weep? (Mark 5:39)
15. Angel, nor spirit: but the ___ confess both. (Acts 23:8)
17. The coat was without seam, woven from the ___ throughout. (John 19:23)
18. Of ___, the family of the Sardites. (Num. 26:26)
19. They are beloved for the ___ sake. (Rom. 11:28)
21. At thy word I will let down the ___. (Luke 5:5)
23. Ye have taken away the ___ of knowledge. (Luke 11:52)
24. May his children be wandering ___. (Ps. 109:10, NIV)
28. Twitch.
32. Salted.
33. I therein do rejoice, ___, and will rejoice. (Phil. 1:18)
35. As he saith also in ___, I will call them my people. (Rom. 9:25)
36. Ye pay ___ of mint and anise and cummin. (Matt. 23:23)
38. Thou art a ___ come from God. (John 3:2)
40. The ___ of all things is at hand. (1 Peter 4:7)
42. I said unto him, ___, thou knowest. (Rev. 7:14)
43. Digit protection.
47. Do not eat the bread of a ___. (Prov. 23:6, NKJ)
51. That ye may be perfect ___ entire. (James 1:4)

52. It rained fire and ___ from heaven. (Luke 17:29)
54. Out of whose womb came the ___? (Job 38:29)
55. Cordelia's father.
56. Of ___, the family of the Eranites. (Num. 26:36)
57. Neptune.
58. He who makes haste with his feet ___. (Prov. 19:2, ASV)
59. The Father ___ the Son to be the Saviour of the world. (1 John 4:14)

Down

1. Girt about the ___ with a golden girdle. (Rev. 1:13)
2. Even in laughter the heart may ___. (Prov. 14:13, NIV)
3. Behold, they that ___ soft clothing are in kings' houses. (Matt. 11:8)
4. Be watchful, and ___ the things which remain. (Rev. 3:2)
5. Straightway forgetteth what manner of man he ___. (James 1:24)
6. Hebrew letter.
7. Cut of meat.
8. To the hungry even what is bitter ___ sweet. (Prov. 27:7, NIV)
9. His violent dealing shall come down upon his ___. (Ps. 7:16)
10. "By this time there is a bad ___." (John 11:39, NIV)
11. Go into the clefts of the rocks, and into the ___ of the ragged rocks. (Isa. 2:21)
16. But you have no ___ where I come from. (John 8:14, NIV)
20. When ye fast, be not, as the ___. (Matt. 6:16)
22. The fire shall ___ every man's work. (1 Cor. 3:13)
24. The heron . . . and the lapwing, and the ___. (Lev. 11:19)
25. The sons of ___, Hophni and Phinehas. (1 Sam. 1:3)

26. The pains of hell ___ hold upon me. (Ps. 116:3)
27. I have ___ before thee an open door. (Rev. 3:8)
29. He planteth an ___, and the rain doth nourish it. (Isa. 44:14)
30. But what went ye out for to ___? (Matt. 11:9)
31. Sea (French).
34. Roman coppers.
37. ___ your servants to speak your word. (Acts 4:29, NIV)
39. An intelligent person ___ at wise action, but a fool starts off in many directions. (Prov. 17:24, GNB)
41. More ominous.

43. His ___ drew the third part of the stars. (Rev. 12:4)
44. Christ also hath ___ suffered for sins. (1 Peter 3:18)
45. Southward were Kabzeel, and ___, and Jagur. (Josh. 15:21)
46. Who is a ___ but he that denieth that Jesus is the Christ? (1 John 2:22)
48. The spirit cried, and rent him ___. (Mark 9:26)
49. Of Naphtali; Ahira the son of ___. (Num. 1:15)
50. The veil of the temple was ___ in twain. (Matt. 27:51)
53. Singular abbreviation of Mesdames.

44

Across

1. This beginning of miracles did Jesus in ___. (John 2:11)
5. Thy King cometh unto thee, meek, and sitting upon an ___. (Matt. 21:5)
8. Asian shrubs.
12. The Arameans think the LORD is ___ [2 words] of the hills. (1 Kings 20:28, NIV)
13. They are ___ with the showers of the mountains. (Job 24:8)
14. I looked, behold a ___ in the wall. (Ezek. 8:7)
15. Watery (comb. form).
16. We sailed to the ___ of Crete. (Acts 27:7, NIV)
17. Operatic solo.
18. My lover is to me a cluster of ___ blossoms. (Song of Sol. 1:14, NIV)
20. We have found the ___, which is, being interpreted the Christ. (John 1:41)
22. A good while ___ God made choice among us. (Acts 15:7)
24. I will ___ my laws into their hearts. (Heb. 10:16)
25. You say to God, "My ___ are flawless." (Job 11:4, NIV)
29. But ran in, and told how ___ stood before the gate. (Acts 12:14)
33. Uzzi, and Ussiel, and Jerimoth, and ___. (1 Chron. 7:7)
34. To silence the ___ and the avenger. (Ps. 8:2, NIV)
36. To set at liberty them that ___ bruised. (Luke 4:18)
37. All the brethren ___ you. (1 Cor. 16:20)
40. They are ___ by a very small rudder. (James 3:4, NIV)
43. The ___ fell upon Matthias. (Acts 1:26)
45. I am like an ___ of the desert. (Ps. 102:6)
46. Unto you is born this day in the city of David a ___. (Luke 2:11)

50. ___ souls were saved by water. (1 Peter 3:20)
54. Nevertheless ___ heart was perfect. (1 Kings 15:14)
55. At the name of Jesus every knee should ___. (Phil. 2:10)
57. Mordecai, the son of ___, the son of Shimei. (Esther 2:5)
58. I am according to thy ___ in God's stead. (Job 33:6)
59. He planteth an ___, and the rain doth nourish it. (Isa. 44:14)
60. Believe ye that I am ___ to do this? (Matt. 9:28)
61. Aztec 'Noah' figure.
62. Rumanian money.
63. Lest he ___ thee to the judge. (Luke 12:58)

Down

1. The priest shall estimate the ___ value. (Lev. 27:18, GNB)
2. Shammah the son of ___. (2 Sam. 23:11)
3. Norse goddess of fate.
4. A name of God.
5. Pierce his ear with an ___. (Exod. 21:6, NIV)
6. If any man among you ___ to be religious (James 1:26)
7. The herd ran violently down a ___ place. (Mark 5:13)
8. They behold your ___ conversation coupled with fear. (1 Peter 3:2)
9. The sons of Lotan; ___, and Homam. (1 Chron. 1:39)
10. Lamb's pseudonym.
11. The seat of God, in the midst of the ___. (Ezek. 28:2)
19. He is of ___; ask him. (John 9:23)
21. I will come in to him, and will ___ with him. (Rev. 3:20)
23. He shook ___ the beast into the fire. (Acts 28:5)
25. He rolled a ___ stone in front of the entrance to the tomb. (Matt. 27:60, NIV)

26. The prophets that make my people ___. (Mic. 3:5)
27. Hath Satan filled thine heart to ___? (Acts 5:3)
28. Naval distress signal.
30. The Valley of Siddim was full of ___ pits. (Gen. 14:10, NIV)
31. Sir, come down ___ my child die. (John 4:49)
32. Behold a great ___ dragon, having seven heads and ten horns. (Rev. 12:3)
35. WW II area.
38. Touched the bones of ___, he revived. (2 Kings 13:21)
39. In all things ye are ___ superstitious. (Acts 17:22)
41. The poor man had nothing, save one little ___ lamb. (2 Sam. 12:3)
42. I will send you ___ the prophet. (Mal. 4:5)

44. ___, and Meshech, they were thy merchants. (Ezek. 27:13)
46. They were stoned, they were ___ asunder. (Heb. 11:37)
47. The churches of ___ salute you. (1 Cor. 16:19)
48. Thus the heavens and the earth were completed in all their ___ array. (Gen. 2:1, NIV)
49. To this end Christ both died, and ___. (Rom. 14:9)
51. Ophni, and ___; twelve cities. (Josh. 18:24)
52. A city that is set on an ___ cannot be hid. (Matt. 5:14)
53. A fig ___ casteth her untimely figs. (Rev. 6:13)
56. ___ are ye fearful, O ye of little faith? (Matt. 8:26)

45

Across

1. Mattathias, which was the son of ___. (Luke 3:25)
5. Hold firmly to the trustworthy message as it ___ been taught. (Titus 1:9, NIV)
8. The poison of ___ is under their lips. (Rom. 3:13)
12. Which are the seven Spirits of God ___ forth into all the earth. (Rev. 5:6)
13. Go to the ___, thou sluggard. (Prov. 6:6)
14. Sendeth ___ on the just and on the unjust. (Matt. 5:45)
15. For he dwelt in the plain of Mamre . . . brother of ___. (Gen. 14:13)
16. Sheepfold.
17. ___, a prophetess, the daughter of Phanuel. (Luke 2:36)
18. Be always ready to give an ___ to every man that asketh you. (1 Peter 3:15)
21. I cannot dig; to ___ I am ashamed. (Luke 16:3)
22. A name of God.
25. Eloi, Eloi, ___ sabachthani? (Mark 15:34)
27. Strong meat belongeth to them that are of full ___. (Heb. 5:14)
28. He was purged from his ___ sins. (2 Peter 1:9)
30. They were all cast in the same ___. (1 Kings 7:37, NIV)
33. It is a ___ thing that the king requireth. (Dan. 2:11)
35. ___ verily, their sound went into all the earth. (Rom. 10:18)
37. I will requite thee in this ___. (2 Kings 9:26)
38. He ___ them all out of the temple. (John 2:15)
40. Military address.
42. Ye all ___ partakers of my grace. (Phil. 1:7)
43. He cannot ___ himself. (2 Tim. 2:13)
45. Let us keep ___[2 words] with the Spirit. (Gal. 5:25, NIV)

Down

47. ___ sent Joram his son unto king David. (2 Sam. 8:10)
49. There went out a ___ from Caesar Augustus. (Luke 2:1)
51. En-gannim, Tappuah, and ___. (Josh. 15:34)
53. Biblical lion.
54. Be not ___ with thy mouth and let not thine heart be hasty. (Eccles. 5:2)
58. Skin disorder.
59. The name of the wicked shall ___. (Prov. 10:7)
60. I am the ___, ye are the branches. (John 15:5)
61. The ___ of the dead lived not again. (Rev. 20:5)
62. Direction: Jerusalem to Hebron [19 miles].
63. Israel journeyed, and spread his tent beyond the tower of ___. (Gen. 35:21)

Down

1. ___ was wroth with the seer. (2 Chron. 16:10)
2. These were redeemed from among ___. (Rev. 14:4)
3. Not as Cain, who was of that wicked ___. (1 John 3:12)
4. The lion shall eat ___ like the bullock. (Isa. 65:25)
5. When Sarai dealt ___ with her, she fled. (Gen. 16:6, NKJ)
6. They are like grass which sprouts ___. (Ps. 90:5, ASV)
7. The bow of ___ shall strike him through. (Job 20:24)
8. Jephunneh, and Pispah, and ___. (1 Chron. 7:38)
9. My God, think thou upon Tobiah and ___. (Neh. 6:14)
10. Our transgressions and our sins be upon us, and we ___ away in them. (Ezek. 33:10)
11. Barb.
19. New (comb. form).
20. Elihu the son of Barachel the Buzite of the kindred of ___. (Job. 32:2)

22. Many pastors have destroyed mine vine ___. (Jer. 12:10)

23. For this ___ is mount Sinai. (Gal. 4:25)

24. The Pharisees . . . took counsel with the ___ against him, how they might destroy him. (Mark 3:6)

26. Cleaning implement.

29. Goddess (Latin).

31. For we ___ not make ourselves of the number. (2 Cor. 10:12)

32. There is but a ___ between me and death. (1 Sam. 20:3)

34. For Adam was first formed, then ___. (1 Tim. 2:13)

36. He cast out the ___ with his word. (Matt. 8:16)

39. Be sober, and hope to the ___ for the grace that is to be brought unto you. (1 Peter 1:13)

41. Thou believest that there is ___ God. (James 2:19)

44. By faith Moses, when he was come to ___. (Heb. 11:24)

46. If any man ___ me, let him follow me. (John 12:26)

47. I, even I, will ___ and go away. (Hos. 5:14)

48. Christ also hath ___ suffered for sins. (1 Peter 3:18)

50. Before the cock ___, thou shalt deny me thrice. (Matt. 26:75)

52. There ___ him ten men that were lepers. (Luke 17:12)

55. You sent me ___ again and again when I was in need. (Phil. 4:16, NIV)

56. Nahoor.

57. But let patience have ___ perfect work. (James 1:4)

46

Across

1. White like wool, as white as ___. (Rev. 1:14)
5. As she sat there nearby, she began to ___. (Gen. 21:16, NIV)
8. Makes dark.
12. Sewing machine inventor.
13. ___, Elah, and Naam [Sons of Caleb]. (1 Chron. 4:15)
14. To the sheltered side.
15. Even the ___ of a meek and quiet spirit. (1 Peter 3:4)
17. His ___ is called The Word of God. (Rev. 19:13)
18. Give unto you the spirit of wisdom and ___. (Eph. 1:17)
20. That by these ye might be partakers of the ___ nature. (2 Peter 1:4)
23. How long will it be ___ they believe? (Num. 14:11)
24. Ram.
25. ___ Lanka.
26. Railroad group (initials).
29. People consult their wooden idol, and their diviner's ___ informs them. (Hos. 4:12, ASV)
30. Omnibus.
31. The roar of rushing waters and like a loud ___ of (Rev. 14:2, NIV)
32. Direction: Masada to Jerusalem [35 miles].
33. Wrath.
34. Draw thee waters for the ___. (Nah. 3:14)
35. Jephunneh, and Pispah, and ___. (1 Chron. 7:38)
36. The heaven departed as a scroll when it is ___ together. (Rev. 6:14)
37. Jesus had made an end of ___ his twelve disciples. (Matt. 11:1)
41. Shammah the son of ___ the Hararite. (2 Sam. 23:11)
42. Do not ___ the throne of thy glory. (Jer. 14:21)

46. Predestined according to the ___ of him who works out everything. (Eph. 1:11, NIV)
47. The serpent beguiled ___ through his subtilty. (2 Cor. 11:3)
48. Whether it is any ___ of wood or clothing or skin or sack. (Lev. 11:32, NKJ)
49. ___ her away; for she crieth after us. (Matt. 15:23)
50. Is this house, which is called by my name, become a ___ of robbers? (Jer. 7:11)
51. There followed him a ___ of meat from the king. (2 Sam. 11:8)

Down

1. Japanese measure.
2. They have no rest day ___ night. (Rev. 14:11)
3. Washed us from our sins in his ___ blood. (Rev. 1:5)
4. Lest ye be ___ and faint in your minds. (Heb. 12:3)
5. Sift the nations with the ___ of vanity. (Isa. 30:28)
6. Trieste Measure.
7. Pharaoh was wroth against two of his officers, against the chief of the ___. (Gen. 40:2)
8. Author of The Divine Comedy .
9. Sibbecai the Hushathite, ___ the Ahohite. (1 Chron. 11:29)
10. Memorandum.
11. He that doeth evil hath not ___ God. (3 John 11)
16. Some ___ sins are open beforehand. (1 Tim. 5:24)
19. Biblical lion.
20. Until the day ___, and the day star arise in your hearts. (2 Peter 1:19)
21. Persia today.
22. The branch cannot bear fruit of itself, except it abide in the ___. (John 15:4)

25. If any man will ___ thee at the law. (Matt. 5:40)
26. They ___ to and fro, and stagger. (Ps. 107:27)
27. Jealousy is the ___ of a man. (Prov. 6:34)
28. Lost blood.
30. Marked by searing.
31. With a multitude that kept a ___ feast. (Ps. 42:4, NKJ)
33. ___ the son of Ikkesh the Tekoite. (2 Sam. 23:26)
34. No man could learn that ___. (Rev. 14:3)

35. Then enquired he of them the hour when he began to ___. (John 4:52)
36. He is not here, but is ___. (Luke 24:6)
37. Make shirts, sashes, and ___ for Aaron's sons. (Exod. 28:40, GNB)
38. Amorous stare.
39. What ___ ye weep and to break mine heart? (Acts 21:13)
40. Headfirst plunge.
43. I ___ no pleasant bread. (Dan. 10:3)
44. French pronoun.
45. German spa.

47

Across

1. The ___ of violence is in their hands. (Isa. 59:6)
4. The earth with her ___ was about me. (Jonah 2:6)
8. ___ hairs are here and there upon him, yet he knoweth not. (Hos. 7:9)
12. Let them shut the doors, and ___ them. (Neh. 7:3)
13. Egyptian month.
14. Germanic letter.
15. Wrath.
16. That ___ is not to the swift. (Eccles. 9:11)
17. The ___ are a people not strong. (Prov. 30:25)
18. Catholic's Revelation.
21. And ___ [2 words] of stumbling, and a rock of offence. (1 Peter 2:8)
23. We passed to the ___ of a small island called Cauda. (Acts 27:16, NIV)
24. Behold, there were ___ in her womb. (Gen. 25:24)
25. She called his name ___ -oni: but his father called him Benjamin. (Gen. 35:18)
26. It doth not ___ appear what we shall be. (1 John 3:2)
29. My couch shall ___ my complaint. (Job 7:13)
30. Put these old rags and worn-out clothes under your arms to ___ the ropes. (Jer. 38:12, NIV)
31. Black-fin snapper.
32. Barley in its place, and ___ within its area. (Isa. 28:25, NIV)
33. Who ___ thou that judgest another man's servant? (Rom. 14:4)
34. But if the ___ be in his sight at a stay. (Lev. 13:37)
35. How long will it be ___ thou be quiet? (Jer. 47:6)
36. God giveth not the ___ by measure unto him. (John 3:34)
37. The ___ of Jesus Christ, which God gave. (Rev. 1:1)
40. As many as I ___, I rebuke. (Rev. 3:19)
41. ___ the Canaanite, which dwelt in the south in the land of Canaan. (Num. 33:40)
42. A man beholding his natural face ___ [2 words] glass. (James 1:23)
45. Zebadiah, and Arad, and ___. (1 Chron. 8:15)
46. Let him ___ the water of life freely. (Rev. 22:17)
47. ___ his son, Jehoshuah his son. (1 Chron. 7:27)
48. Though I should die with thee, yet will I not ___ thee. (Matt. 26:35)
49. Unto Shem also, the father of all the children of ___. (Gen. 10:21)
50. Buy and sell, and ___ gain. (James 4:13)

Down

1. His mother's name also was ___. (2 Kings 18:2)
2. Pursued the Philistines, and smote them, until they came under Beth-___. (1 Sam. 7:11)
3. The former ___ have I made, O Theophilus. (Acts 1:1)
4. Feudal lords.
5. Kings of armies did flee ___. (Ps. 68:12)
6. Whosoever shall say to his brother, ___, shall be in danger of the council. (Matt. 5:22)
7. Relieved another.
8. Drink the pure blood of the ___. (Deut. 32:14)
9. The man ___ away because he is a hired hand. (John 10:13, NIV)
10. Previous in time (prefix).
11. ___, of the Gentiles also. (Rom. 3:29)
19. Cornmeal patty.
20. Craving for

21. The children of ___ of Hezekiah. (Ezra 2:16)
22. On the tops of the hills may it ___. (Ps. 72:16, NIV)
25. The lapwing, and the ___. (Lev. 11:19)
26. Where are Your zeal and Your strength, the ___ of Your heart? (Isa. 63:15, NIV)
27. Naum, which was the son of ___. (Luke 3:25)
28. Who is wise enough to count the clouds and ___ them over to pour out the rain. (Job 38:37, GNB)
30. Bishop.
31. Alternate spelling of Chios (see Acts 20:15).
33. In whom ___ hid all the treasures of wisdom. (Col. 2:3)

34. The ___ taketh hold with her hands. (Prov. 30:28)
35. To give ___ man according as his work. (Rev. 22:12)
36. Reconsider, for my integrity is at ___. (Job. 6:29, NIV)
37. He ___ upon a cherub, and did fly. (Ps. 18:10)
38. ___ so, come, Lord Jesus. (Rev. 22:20)
39. ___, and Dumah, and Eshean. (Josh. 15:52)
40. There is a ___ here, which hath five barley loaves and two small fishes. (John 6:9)
43. The day that ___ entered into the ark. (Matt. 24:38)
44. Go to the ___, thou sluggard. (Prov. 6:6)

97

48

Across

1. Our eyelids ___ out with waters. (Jer. 9:18)
5. When Agrippa was come, and Bernice, with great ___. (Acts 25:23)
9. I saw Absalom hanged in an ___. (2 Sam. 18:10)
12. Sibbecai the Hushathite, ___ the Ahohite. (1 Chron. 11:29)
13. To affirm.
14. The wheat and the ___ were not smitten. (Exod. 9:32)
15. Rejoicing, so that the city ___ again. (1 Kings 1:45)
16. Timor's neighbor.
17. For if they do these things in a green tree, what shall be done in the ___? (Luke 23:31)
18. They are altogether ___ than vanity. (Ps. 62:9)
20. British health program.
22. Abstain from fleshly lusts, which ___ against the soul. (1 Peter 2:11)
23. He ___ the battle from afar. (Job 39:25, ASV)
26. The sons of Bela were, ___, and Gera. (1 Chron. 8:3)
29. We sailed to the ___ of Crete. (Acts 27:7, NIV)
30. There was seen in his temple the ___ of his testament. (Rev. 11:19)
31. Suffer me first go and ___ my father. (Luke 9:59)
32. Naphtali is a ___ set free. (Gen. 49:21, NIV)
33. ___hair the splendor of the old. (Prov. 20:29, NIV)
34. Sir, come down ___ my child die (John 4:49)
35. Lord, let it alone this year also, till I shall ___ about it, and dung it. (Luke 13:8)
36. More cunning.
37. The sons of Gershonite ___, chief fathers. (1 Chron. 26:21)
39. Japanese dry measure.
40. They ___ my path, they set forward my calamity, they have no helper. (Job 30:13)

41. What shall I do that I may inherit ___ life? (Mark 10:17)
45. I took the little book out of the angel's hand, and ___ it up. (Rev. 10:10)
47. Writing (Japanese).
49. 'Pompeii' character.
50. ___, we would see Jesus. (John 12:21)
51. Of ___, the family of the Eranites. (Num. 26:36)
52. ___, which was the son of Seth, which was the son of Adam, which was the son of God. (Luke 3:38)
53. Common contraction (masc.).
54. The seven thin ears devoured the seven ___ and full ears. (Gen. 41:7)
55. The angel Gabriel was ___ from God. (Luke 1:26)

Down

1. A boy for an harlot, and sold a ___ for wine, that they might drink. (Joel 3:3)
2. In a vision, and I was by the river of ___. (Dan. 8:2)
3. Paul and Silas prayed, and ___ praises. (Acts 16:25)
4. The son of Timaeus sat by the ___ side begging. (Mark 10:46)
5. In his distress King Belshazzar grew even ___. (Dan. 5:9, GNB)
6. Obey them that have the rule ___ you. (Heb. 13:17)
7. A certain damsel possessed with a spirit of divination ___ us. (Acts 16:16)
8. The ___ of this world is judged. (John 16:11)
9. And have diminished thine ___ food. (Ezek. 16:27)
10. Ye shall speak into the ___. (1 Cor. 14:9)
11. Ye have taken away the ___ of knowledge. (Luke 11:52)
19. She got a papyrus basket for him and coated it with ___ and pitch. (Exod. 2:3, NIV)
21. ___ that wavereth is like a wave of the sea. (James 1:6)

23. Now we ___ through a glass, darkly. (1 Cor. 13:12)
24. Whom they slew and hanged on a ___. (Acts 10:39)
25. Bonnyclabber.
26. By faith ___ offered unto God a more excellent sacrifice. (Heb. 11:4)
27. The king made an image of gold . . . he set it up in the plain of ___. (Dan. 3:1)
28. These filthy ___ defile the flesh. (Jude 8)
29. Mingled with oil, and one ___ of oil. (Lev. 14:10)
32. He will silence her noisy ___. (Jer. 51:55, NIV)
33. He predicted the sufferings of Christ and the ___ that would follow. (1 Peter 1:11, NIV)
35. His eyes will be ___ than wine. (Gen. 49:12, NIV)

36. ___ had received the spies with peace. (Heb. 11:31)
38. Yes (Russian).
39. It [manna] bred worms, and ___. (Exod. 16:20)
41. Naphtali was Ahira the son of ___. (Num. 10:27)
42. Thank God that I baptized ___ of you. (1 Cor. 1:14)
43. The same is he that heareth the word, and ___ with joy receiveth it. (Matt. 13:20)
44. Beware ___ any man spoil you. (Col. 2:8)
45. Among the trees of the forest, he planteth an ___. (Isa. 44:14)
46. Now therefore make a new cart, and ___ the kine to the cart. (1 Sam. 6:7)
48. Jephunneh, and Pispah, and ___. (1 Chron. 7:38)

49

Across

1. ___ herself received strength to conceive. (Heb. 11:11)
5. Thou shalt in any wise let the ___ go. (Deut. 22:7)
8. The earth and the heaven ___ away. (Rev. 20:11)
12. Elderly.
13. We know not: he is of ___; ask him. (John 9:21)
14. Take thine ___, eat, drink, and be merry. (Luke 12:19)
15. The city had no ___ of the sun. (Rev. 21:23)
16. His servant Joshua, the son of ___. (Exod. 33:11)
17. Manner of.
18. I am set for the ___ of the gospel. (Phil. 1:17)
20. They sat down in ___, by hundreds and by fifties. (Mark 6:40)
21. Upon the great ___ of their right foot. (Exod. 29:20)
22. Bore his ear through with an ___. (Exod. 21:6)
23. The angel which appeared to him in the ___. (Acts 7:35)
26. Dead Sea Scrolls writers.
30. Abia begat ___. (Matt. 1:7)
31. That they ___ be judged according to men in the flesh. (1 Peter 4:6)
33. ___ no man anything. (Rom. 13:8)
34. The ___ of treasures by a lying tongue is a vanity. (Prov. 21:6)
36. Do works ___ for repentance. (Acts 26:20)
37. At that day ye shall ___ in my name. (John 16:26)
38. Why make ye this ___, and weep? (Mark 5:39)
40. The Holy Spirit ___ me that prison and hardships are facing me. (Acts 20:23, NIV)
43. ___, and Lachish, and Azekah. (2 Chron. 11:9)
47. Their conscience seared with a hot ___. (1 Tim. 4:2)

48. A good while ___ God made choice among us. (Acts 15:7)
49. Their words seemed to them as ___ tales (Luke 24:11)
50. Which ___ professing have erred concerning the faith. (1 Tim. 6:21)
51. Neither shalt thou ___ the corners of thy beard. (Lev. 19:27)
52. And Ahijah, Hanan, ___. (Neh. 10:26)
53. Mahli, and ___, and Jeremoth. (1 Chron. 24:30)
54. Wrath.
55. Parrot hawks.

Down

1. A foolish man, which built his house upon the ___. (Matt. 7:26)
2. Shammah the son of ___. (2 Sam. 23:11)
3. Striking a ___ where two seas met. (Acts 27:41, ASV)
4. If it be confirmed, no man disannulleth, or ___ thereto. (Gal. 3:15)
5. Praise him with the timbrel and ___. (Ps. 150:4)
6. Consumption, and the burning ___. (Lev. 26:16)
7. Honour all ___. Love the brotherhood. (1 Peter 2:17)
8. At the beginning made them male and ___. (Matt. 19:4)
9. He had ___ in the grave four days already. (John 11:17)
10. He called the name of the well ___. (Gen. 26:20)
11. Hid themselves in the ___ and in the rocks. (Rev. 6:15)
19. Art thou better than populous ___. (Nahum 3:8)
20. The ___ of them shall be a witness against you. (James 5:3)
22. He planteth an ___. (Isa. 44:14)
23. He was a thief, and had the ___. (John 12:6)
24. ___ a little wine for thy stomach's sake. (1 Tim. 5:23)

25. Jesus ___ over against the treasury. (Mark 12:41)
26. Or if he shall ask an ___, will he offer him a scorpion? (Luke 11:12)
27. As the days of ___ were. (Matt. 24:37)
28. Abraham set seven ___ lambs of the flock by themselves. (Gen. 21:28)
29. I have ___ before thee an open door. (Rev. 3:8)
31. If my father at all ___ me. (1 Sam. 20:6)
32. Written not with ___, but with the Spirit of the living God. (2 Cor. 3:3)
35. He lodgeth with one Simon a ___. (Acts 10:6)
36. Get thee into the land of ___. (Gen. 22:2)
38. How right you are to ___ you. (Song of Sol. 1:4, NIV)

39. For if you ___ these things you will never fall. (2 Peter 1:10)
40. The holy scriptures, which are able to make thee ___ unto salvation. (2 Tim. 3:15)
41. ___, the family of the Arodites. (Num. 26:17)
42. Commanded all Jews to depart from ___. (Acts 18:2)
43. Which gendereth to bondage, which is ___. (Gal. 4:24)
44. Of Harim, ___; of Meraioth, Helkai. (Neh. 12:15)
45. ___ the Ahohite. (1 Chron. 11:29)
46. Having ___ persons in admiration because of advantage. (Jude 16)
48. Zebaim, the children of ___. (Ezra 2:57)

50

Across

1. He hath by inheritance obtained a more excellent name than ___. (Heb. 1:4)
5. The dumb ___ speaking with man's voice. (2 Peter 2:16)
8. They which could ___ should cast themselves first into the sea. (Acts 27:43)
12. Speak, ye that ___ on white asses. (Judg. 5:10)
13. Woe to the women that ___ pillows. (Ezek. 13:18)
14. Your moon will ___ no more. (Isa. 60:20, NIV)
15. Their ___ of pleasure is to carouse. (2 Peter 2:13, NIV)
16. Cast out the wheat into the ___. (Acts 27:38)
17. Low female voice.
18. I return to fight with the prince of ___. (Dan. 10:20)
20. A dove covered with silver, and her feathers with ___ gold. (Ps. 68:13)
22. He that sat upon him was called Faithful and ___. (Rev. 19:11)
24. Lines.
25. That which groweth of ___ own accord. (Lev. 25:5)
28. Our Lord Jesus Christ be with you ___. (Rev. 22:21)
29. Like a slug melting away as it ___ along. (Ps. 58:8, NIV)
33. I will ___ out in those days of my Spirit. (Acts 2:18)
35. Sesame.
37. John ___ clothing made of camel's hair. (Mark 1:6, NIV)
38. He touched the hollow of Jacob's thigh in the ___ that shrank. (Gen. 32:32)
40. Here am I, and the children God ___ given me. (Heb. 2:13, NIV)
42. They are ___ with the showers of the mountains. (Job 24:8)
43. Tramp.

44. The body is a ___. (1 Cor. 12:12, NIV)
46. When ye come into an house, ___ it. (Matt. 10:12)
50. Sit on thrones judging the twelve ___ of Israel. (Luke 22:30)
54. He called the name of the well ___. (Gen. 26:20)
55. To live is Christ, and to ___ is gain. (Phil. 1:21)
57. Did all eat the same spiritual ___. (1 Cor. 10:3)
58. Ireland.
59. Ye do ___, not knowing the scriptures. (Matt. 22:29)
60. Repent, or ___ I will come unto thee quickly. (Rev. 2:16)
61. Girt about the ___ with a golden girdle. (Rev. 1:13)
62. The LORD spake unto Joshua the son of ___. (Josh. 1:1)
63. For sin deceived me, . . . and by it ___ me. (Rom. 7:11)

Down

1. Men of violence who plan to ___ my feet. (Ps. 140:4, NIV)
2. ___ us from the face of him that sitteth on the throne. (Rev. 6:16)
3. Mahli, and ___, and Jeremoth, three. (1 Chron. 23:23)
4. Watch out for the ___ of the Pharisees. (Mark 8:15, NIV)
5. There was an ___ made both of the Gentiles, and also of the Jews. (Acts 14:5)
6. Whereas I was blind, now I ___. (John 9:25)
7. On the tops of the hills may it ___. (Ps. 72:16, NIV)
8. Strain at a gnat, and ___ a camel. (Matt. 23:24)
9. God shall smite thee, thou whited ___. (Acts 23:3)
10. Which things the angels desire to look.___. (1 Peter 1:12)
11. Cat call.

19. ___ the son of Ikkesh the Tekoite. (2 Sam. 23:26)
21. Wood mentioned in Hosea 4:13.
23. ___ had waited till Job had spoken. (Job 32:4)
25. Distance/time abbreviation.
26. ___ king of Hamath. (2 Sam. 8:9)
27. Let not the ___ go down upon your wrath. (Eph. 4:26)
30. ___, and pay unto the LORD your God. (Ps. 76:11)
31. How long will it be ___ they believe me? (Num. 14:11)
32. Nature; and it is ___ on fire of hell. (James 3:6)
34. When thou with ___ dost correct man for iniquity, thou makest his beauty. (Ps. 39:11)
36. Light carrier.
39. ___ ye not what the scripture saith? (Rom. 11:2)

41. ___, didst not thou sow good seed? (Matt. 13:27)
45. Hath in due ___ manifested his word through preaching. (Titus 1:3)
46. Ooze through.
47. The churches of ___ salute you. (1 Cor. 16:19)
48. Sweet secretion.
49. The land of Nod, on the east of ___. (Gen. 4:16)
51. A pomegranate, a golden ___ and a pomegranate upon the hem of the robe. (Exod. 28:34)
52. Woe to them that are at ___ in Zion. (Amos 6:1)
53. Jacob gave Esau some bread and some lentil ___. (Gen. 25:34, NIV)
56. The sons of Caleb the son of Jephunneh; ___, Elah, and Naam. (1 Chron. 4:15)

Answers

1

```
A D A M   G O D   S L A B
M A R A   O N E   H A R E
O R E N   V I E   A G E E
S T A N C E   P E R S O N
      E U R   E N D
B A R R E N   R E S C U E
I R A             A S A
D E M O T E   M E M B E R
      T E N   U R I
M O T H E R   R E L I E F
A L E E   I A M   C O A L
S E A R   C R U   A N T A
H O R S   H A R   H A S T
```

4

```
A R A B   A R E A   H A S
S O S O   R A A B   A D O
S E P T E M B E R   M A N
      T R Y   A D A M S
A R M O R   A S H E N
N O R M   B A H A I   G O
N O S   L O R A M   M A W
A T   T A L O N   T A L L
    D O Z E N   C A L L S
D I A N A   A I N
A R M   R E A D I N E S S
R A N   U R G E   E A S E
E M S   S E E R   D R E W
```

2

```
L A W   A H O Y   G R I P
E N E   D E M E   R I D E
A N T   D R E W   I D E A
P A S S I O N   A N
    E N D   A N D R E W
S W I N G   S P Y   A C E
H I L T   S A T   A G H A
O L A   H E W   S H E O L
O L I V E T   A P E
    A M   P R O M I S E
M A I L   L O O K   N E T
E S A U   E L S E   T E N
T A M E   T E E N   O N A
```

5

```
B A L L   S A N G   G O B
A L I E   A S I A   O W E
R E N A   V E E R   O L D
R E E D S E A   D I D
      E E S   K E N N E L
C O B R A   D I N   E S E
O N E S   W O N   S W A T
I T A   S I R   J E S U S
N O U G H T   M O A
      T O O   S A B B A T H
E L I   U L A I   E R I E
H O E   L E N D   E A R L
I T S   D O G S   S H O P
```

3

```
B E T A   P L A Y   A G O
A D I N   R I T E   G A D
D O C T R I N E S   E V E
      I O N E   D E E D
E L I C I T   E L I
B A T H S   C R O O K E D
B I E R   L E E   T A X I
S C R I B E S   T R I E S
      S E T   F R E N C H
W E S T   G R I P
I V E   H O L Y G H O S T
D E N   I N E E   E L O I
E N D   D O E R   S E W N
```

6

```
A P T   Z I B A   L E N D
N O E   I S L E   A S I A
A S S   M A A I   S A N S
K E T U R A H   S H U A H
      S A C   W O E
S A L E M   J O K S H A N
E L A   R A T   E R E
A B R A H A M   I S L E S
      B E N   A S E
M E D A N   I S H M A E L
A M O S   A B I B   H A E
R I T E   V I D A   A S A
S T E S   E S E K   B E D
```

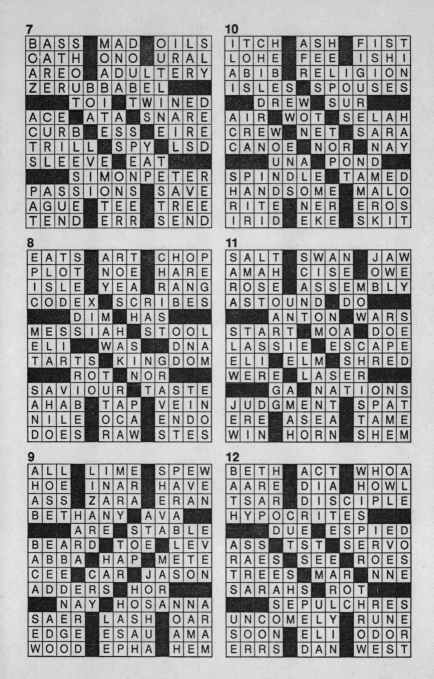

13

W	E	B		S	I	N	G		S	O	A	P
H	A	E		H	A	I	R		P	A	G	E
I	C	E		R	O	P	E		I	R	O	N
T	H	R	E	E		S	E	A	R			
			A	W	E		T	H	I	N	K	S
R	A	M		D	A	M		A	T	O	N	E
A	N	E	W		R	A	N		S	N	O	W
S	T	E	A	L		H	E	R		O	W	N
H	A	T	R	E	D		W	A	S			
			N	E	E	D		I	S	L	E	S
I	L	A	I		A	I	M	S		O	N	E
T	O	R	N		T	R	E	E		S	O	N
S	T	A	G		H	E	L	D		E	S	T

16

L	O	T		E	D	A	R		A	M	O	S
E	A	R		L	E	N	E		G	E	N	E
E	R	E		I	C	O	N		R	A	C	E
	S	E	C	O	N	D	P	E	T	E	R	
R	E	P	A	I	R		E	Y	E			
E	N	A	C	T		T	R	E		S	H	Y
B	O	S	H		S	O	S		C	H	O	P
A	S	S		S	A	P		N	A	O	M	I
			A	I	M		S	A	M	U	E	L
F	I	R	S	T	S	A	M	U	E	L		
A	D	A	H		O	L	I	G		D	A	M
L	E	T	E		N	A	T	H		E	N	E
L	A	S	S		S	T	E	T		R	A	N

14

W	A	G		A	I	J	A		O	A	K	S
I	R	A		C	R	O	P		U	N	I	T
T	A	R	S	H	I	S	H		T	A	L	E
		H	E		H	I	L	L	T	O	P	
G	R	A	Y		J	U	D	E	A			
A	I	L		B	O	A		A	S	S	E	T
M	E	A	S	L	Y		E	S	T	H	E	R
E	L	I	H	U		S	A	T		O	N	O
			E	S	T	E	R		T	E	S	T
B	I	G	T	H	A	N		A	I			
A	D	A	H		M	O	R	D	E	C	A	I
A	L	T	A		A	R	E	A		A	R	C
L	E	E	R		R	A	I	N		B	E	E

15

I	L	L		A	H	A	B		A	M	A	H
S	E	E		R	I	P	E		C	A	R	E
U	S	E		B	L	E	D		H	A	I	R
I	S	R	A	E	L	S		S	A	R	D	S
			S	L	Y		I	I	I			
J	O	P	P	A		A	B	R	A	H	A	M
O	N	E		S	R	O		O	N	O		
G	A	L	I	L	E	E		C	U	R	S	E
			S	O	W		H	A	D			
S	T	A	R	T		G	E	R	I	Z	I	M
H	A	R	A		A	R	A	M		I	R	A
A	L	E	E		H	A	V	E		B	A	N
M	E	A	L		A	B	E	L		A	N	Y

17

T	R	Y		R	A	C	A		S	P	R	Y
H	O	E		E	L	A	H		T	H	E	E
U	S	A		M	A	R	A		R	I	D	S
S	E	R	V	A	N	T		B	A	L		
			E	R	D		B	O	W	E	L	S
S	T	O	R	K		S	A	Y		M	O	W
T	I	N	Y		D	A	N		B	O	N	A
A	R	E		S	O	W		H	O	N	E	Y
R	E	S	C	U	E		G	O	O			
			I	O	N		B	R	O	T	H	E	R
A	T	M	O		G	O	A	D		E	V	E
P	A	U	L		O	N	C	E		L	I	E
T	E	S	S		D	E	E	D		I	L	L

18

P	I	P	E		S	A	D		R	A	L	E
A	L	A	S		E	R	R		O	L	E	S
C	A	S	T		T	I	E		M	E	A	L
T	I	T	H	E		M	A	L	A	C	H	I
			E	R	A		M	E	N			
A	N	D	R	E	W	S		E	S	H	E	K
S	O	O		E	A	T		A	T	I		
S	A	R	A	H		T	R	I	M	M	E	D
			B	O	T		Y	O	U			
H	E	B	R	E	W	S		U	T	T	E	R
E	Z	R	A		I	N	N		T	A	R	E
R	E	A	M		S	O	E		E	L	I	S
A	R	T	S		T	W	O		R	E	N	T

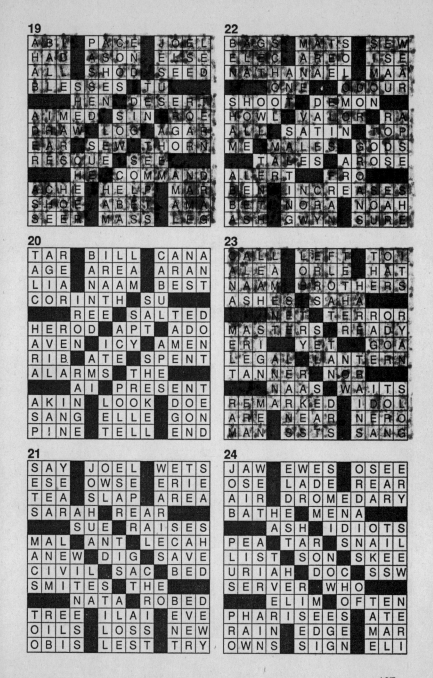

19

```
ABI  PACE  JOEL
HAD  ASON  ELSE
ALL  SHOD  SEED
BLESSES   TU
     HEN  DESERT
AIMED  SIN  ROE
DRAW  LOG  AGAR
EAR  SEW  THORN
RESCUE   SEE
     HE  COMMAND
ACHE  HELP  MAR
SHOE  ABES  AMA
SEER  MASS  LEG
```

22

```
BAGS  MATS  SEW
ELEC  AREO  ISE
NATHANAEL  MAA
     ONE  ODOUR
SHOOT   DEMON
HOWL  VALOR  RA
ALI  SATIN  TOP
ME  MALES  GODS
     TALES  AROSE
ALERT   FRO
BEN  INCREASES
BET  NORA  NOAH
ASH  GWYN  SURE
```

20

```
TAR  BILL  CANA
AGE  AREA  ARAN
LIA  NAAM  BEST
CORINTH   SU
     REE  SALTED
HEROD  APT  ADO
AVEN  ICY  AMEN
RIB  ATE  SPENT
ALARMS   THE
     AI  PRESENT
AKIN  LOOK  DOE
SANG  ELLE  GON
PINE  TELL  END
```

23

```
CALL   LEFT  TOI
ALEA  ORLE  HAT
NAAM  BROTHERS
ASHES  SAHA
     NET  TERROR
MASTERS  READY
ERI   YET  GOA
LEGAL  LANTERN
TANNER  NOB
     NAAS  WAITS
REMARKED  IDOL
ARE  NEAR  NERO
MAN  SSTS  SANG
```

21

```
SAY  JOEL  WETS
ESE  OWSE  ERIE
TEA  SLAP  AREA
SARAH  REAR
     SUE  RAISES
MAL  ANT  LECAH
ANEW  DIG  SAVE
CIVIL  SAC  BED
SMITES   THE
     NATA  ROBED
TREE  ILAI  EVE
OILS  LOSS  NEW
OBIS  LEST  TRY
```

24

```
JAW  EWES  OSEE
OSE  LADE  REAR
AIR  DROMEDARY
BATHE  MENA
     ASH  IDIOTS
PEA  TAR  SNAIL
LIST  SON  SKEE
URIAH  DOC  SSW
SERVER  WHO
     ELIM  OFTEN
PHARISEES  ATE
RAIN  EDGE  MAR
OWNS  SIGN  ELI
```

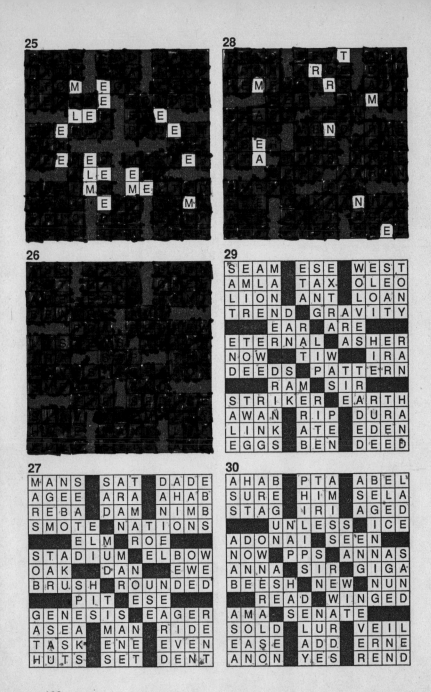

25

28

26

29

S	E	A	M		E	S	E		W	E	S	T
A	M	L	A		T	A	X		O	L	E	O
L	I	O	N		A	N	T		L	O	A	N
T	R	E	N	D		G	R	A	V	I	T	Y
		E	A	R		A	R	E				
E	T	E	R	N	A	L		A	S	H	E	R
N	O	W		T	I	W		I	R	A		
D	E	E	D	S		P	A	T	T	E	R	N
		R	A	M		S	I	R				
S	T	R	I	K	E	R		E	A	R	T	H
A	W	A	N		R	I	P		D	U	R	A
L	I	N	K		A	T	E		E	D	E	N
E	G	G	S		B	E	N		D	E	E	D

27

M	A	N	S		S	A	T		D	A	D	E
A	G	E	E		A	R	A		A	H	A	B
R	E	B	A		D	A	M		N	I	M	B
S	M	O	T	E		N	A	T	I	O	N	S
		E	L	M		R	O	E				
S	T	A	D	I	U	M		E	L	B	O	W
O	A	K		D	A	N		E	W	E		
B	R	U	S	H		R	O	U	N	D	E	D
		P	I	T		E	S	E				
G	E	N	E	S	I	S		E	A	G	E	R
A	S	E	A		M	A	N		R	I	D	E
T	A	S	K		E	N	E		E	V	E	N
H	U	T	S		S	E	T		D	E	N	T

30

A	H	A	B		P	T	A		A	B	E	L
S	U	R	E		H	I	M		S	E	L	A
S	T	A	G		I	R	I		A	G	E	D
		U	N	L	E	S	S		I	C	E	
A	D	O	N	A	I		S	E	E	N		
N	O	W		P	P	S		A	N	N	A	S
A	N	N	A		S	I	R		G	I	G	A
B	E	E	S	H		N	E	W		N	U	N
		R	E	A	D		W	I	N	G	E	D
A	M	A		S	E	N	A	T	E			
S	O	L	D		L	U	R		V	E	I	L
E	A	S	E		A	D	D		E	R	N	E
A	N	O	N		Y	E	S		R	E	N	D

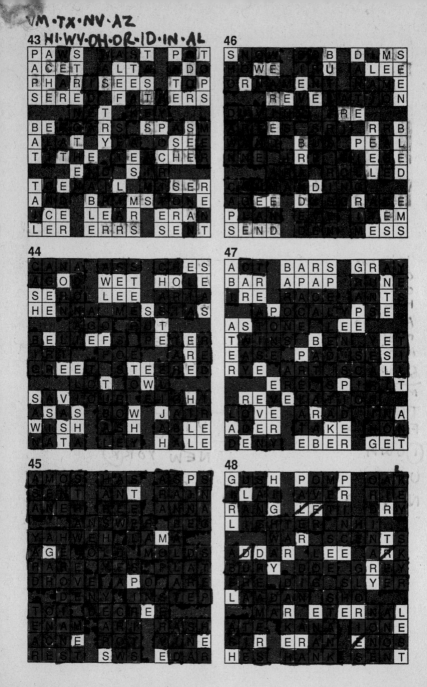

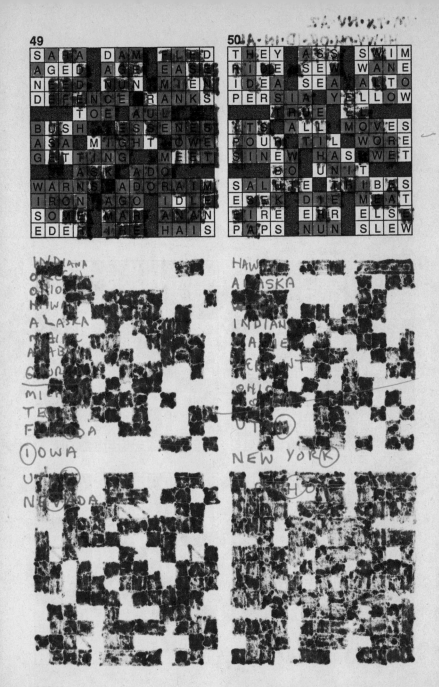

49

S	A	R	A		D	A	M		F	L	E	D
A	G	E	D		A	C	E		E	A	S	E
N	E	E	D		N	U	N		M	I	E	N
D	E	F	E	N	C	E		R	A	N	K	S
			T	O	E		A	U				
B	U	S	H		S	S	E	N	E	S		
A	S	A		M	I	G	H	T		O	W	E
G	E	T	T	I	N	G		M	E	E	T	
		A	S	K		A	D	O				
W	A	R	N	S		A	D	O	R	A	I	M
I	R	O	N		A	G	O		I	D	L	E
S	O	M	E		M	A	R		A	N	A	N
E	D	E	F		I	C	E		H	A	I	S

50

T	H	E	Y		A	S	S		S	W	I	M
R	I	D	E		S	E	W		W	A	N	E
I	D	E	A		S	E	A		A	L	T	O
P	E	R	S	I	A		Y	E	L	L	O	W
			T	R	U	E						
I	T	S		A	L	L		M	O	V	E	S
P	O	U	T		T	I	L		W	O	R	E
S	I	N	E	W		H	A	S	E	W	E	T
		B	O		U	N	I	T				
S	A	L	U	T	E		T	R	I	B	E	S
E	S	E	K		D	I	E		M	E	A	T
F	I	R	E		E	R	R		E	L	S	E
P	A	P	S		N	U	N		S	L	E	W

INDIANA
OREGON
OHIO
HAWAII
ALASKA
MAINE
ALABAMA
GEORGIA
MICHIGAN
TEXAS
FLORIDA
(I)OWA
UTAH
NEVADA

HAWAII
ALASKA

INDIANA
MAINE
VERMONT
OHIO
UTAH
NEW YORK
OHIO